A PAST and PRESENT Compani

C000231410

The
GREAT CENTRAL RAILWAY
Nottingham to Rugby
Past and Present

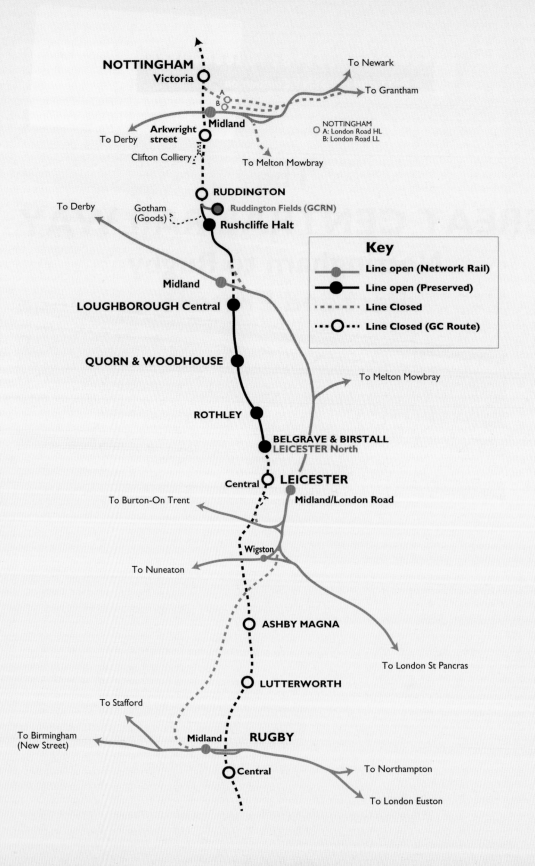

NOTTINGHAM
Victoria

To Newark

To Grantham

A
B
Midland

NOTTINGHAM
A: London Road HL
B: London Road LL

Arkwright street

To Derby

Clifton Colliery

To Melton Mowbray

RUDDINGTON

To Derby

Gotham (Goods)

Ruddington Fields (GCRN)

Rushcliffe Halt

Midland

Key

━━⬤━━	**Line open (Network Rail)**
━━⬤━━	**Line open (Preserved)**
┈┈┈┈	**Line Closed**
┈┈○┈┈	**Line Closed (GC Route)**

LOUGHBOROUGH Central

QUORN & WOODHOUSE

To Melton Mowbray

ROTHLEY

BELGRAVE & BIRSTALL
LEICESTER North

Central

LEICESTER

To Burton-On Trent

Midland/London Road

Wigston

To Nuneaton

ASHBY MAGNA

To London St Pancras

LUTTERWORTH

To Stafford

To Birmingham (New Street)

Midland

RUGBY

Central

To Northampton

To London Euston

A PAST and PRESENT Companion

The
GREAT CENTRAL RAILWAY
Nottingham to Rugby
Past and Present

John Stretton

Past & Present Publishing Ltd

First published in 2014
Reprinted in 2015

British Library Cataloguing in Publication Data
A catalogue record for this book is available from the
British Library.

Softcover: ISBN 978 1 85895 265 9
Hardcover: ISBN 978 1 85895 286 4

Past & Present Publishing Ltd
The Trundle
Ringstead Road
Great Addington
Kettering
Northants
NN14 4BW

Tel/Fax: 01536 330588

email: sales@nostalgiacollection.com

Website: www.nostalgiacollection.com

Printed and bound in the Czech Republic

Acknowledgements

As always, I am indebted to a wide variety and number
of people who have assisted in one way or another.
Photographers, especially, have been very willing to
submit their images for consideration and I am truly
grateful to those who aided in this way – without them
and their foresight in pointing the camera at strategic
moments the book would have struggled to be born!
They are duly credited throughout the collection,
but I take this opportunity to offer all of them my
profound gratitude. In addition, there are those who
have helped me before and have been fool enough
to put their name in the frame again! Amongst all of
these there are some who deserve especial mention,
and I would like to here present my sincere thanks
to (in no particular order): David Richards, G. D.
King, Peter Johnson, Marian Thwaites, Colin Nash (of
Milepost 92½), Mike Mensing, Mike Mitchell, Bryan
Jennings, Barry Hilton, Jan Morgan, Bryan Hicks, Peter
Simmonds, Syd Hancock, John Keylock, Nigel Harris
(for his Foreword), Chris Williams (for proofreading),
Six Bells Junction.co.uk, Colour-Rail and various staff
members of the present GCR. Finally, as usual, thanks
go to all at Silver Link – Peter for encouragement and
for putting up with countless phone calls, and David
and Will for their unflinching patience and courtesy.
Thank you all! The illustrations credited MJS are mine.

Contents

BELGRAVE & BIRSTALL: Great things are often achieved by persons of vision, passion and enthusiasm. One who can rightly lay claim to these attributes is Ian Allan, without whom the world of trainspotting and present-day rail enthusiasm would probably not have been born. His 'Locospotters Club' excursions took participants and locomotives to many an unlikely place but, perhaps, none as unexpected as an 'A4' 'Pacific' to Belgrave & Birstall station. On 24 April 1957 No 60029 *Woodcock* steams into the station on its way to Doncaster Works, from Paddington via Princes Risborough. Sadly, it failed at Nottingham Victoria on the return journey! *G. D. King*

I was delighted when John Stretton asked me to write a Foreword to this book. I've always had a 'soft spot' for the 'Past & Present' series, not merely because I started publishing it during my own 'Silver Link Publishing' days, but also because I co-authored the very first volume, way back in 1985, with John Broughton.

At that time Silver Link was a new, small publisher looking for ideas. In my time in Kendal, on the *Westmorland Gazette* as a trainee reporter (1979-81), I'd been given the 'Now and Then' series to compile. It was comparison of old and new pictures around Kendal and the South Lakes and I'd enjoyed doing it immensely. It was a really popular feature in the weekly paper, so I'd floated the idea with a local publisher long before SLP was launched. Later, with the new company up and running, it seemed a natural project for SLP.

I asked John B. to cover half the shoots required (and the photo printing – he was an ace darkroom man) and off we went. It was such fun – and I'm sure the many other P&P authors would agree. It is not as easy as you might think, and getting in the right position (and even finding it, sometimes) is challenging. I found some of the shoots especially sad. I shall never forget standing in the scrub at what was left of lovely little Penruddock station on the 'CK&P' route through the Lake District. In my hand, one of Derek Cross's pictures of a special train in the once-neat little station – in front of me a wasteland of dereliction and abandonment.

The book stormed off the shelf – the series was off to a blazing start. And here we are, 29 years later, with almost 100 volumes in the main and 'Companion' series! John S. does me a great honour in asking me to write this Foreword, because the GCR route is close to my heart. I've always been interested in the last, lost main line since I read an Ian Allan *Trains Illustrated* annual years ago about an old chap witnessing its closure as a through route in 1966, having watched

LUTTERWORTH: The default design for stations on the northern stretch of the railway covered by this book was an island arrangement, with a central stairway access from an adjacent road, mostly from above. Lutterworth was one of the less common type, being accessed from the road below, rather than an overbridge. The central staircase rose from the road and the platform extended across the road bridge. The glass-sided structure on the right protects the top of the stairwell from the worst of the weather. Seen on 15 August 1955, looking north towards Leicester, holiday trips to Boston, Skegness, Sutton-on-Sea and Mablethorpe are advertised, although the vast majority of Leicestershire trippers would be travelling to these from Leicester (Belgrave Road) station. *Milepost 92½, railphotolibrary.com*

the opening in 1899 as a young boy. Yes, a whole main line had been born, lived and died in a single human lifetime. That fact still resonates. Like the fact that in the mid-1960s Prime Minister Harold Wilson was in France talking to President de Gaulle about a Channel Tunnel, while back home Transport Minister Barbara Castle was closing the Berne Gauge main line built to serve precisely such a tunnel, which had been envisioned by the GCR in the previous century. Joined-up Government, eh?

Still, part of the GCR survives and I'm proud to be a steam driver on the Loughborough-Leicester section (so wonderfully covered in these pages), and I'm also Chairman of GCR Development Ltd, set up in 2010 to reconnect the GCR with the GCR(N), the Nottingham-Loughborough section. So I found plenty to fascinate and entertain in this book – as I know you will too. As I write these words I've just left a meeting with Network Rail, which we've contracted to reinstate the bridge over the Midland Main Line you'll see on page 34. It's scheduled to be back in place by 2015.

This is a great book, so well done to John for this volume and to SLP for making such a success of the P&P series. It's been a privilege to write this and in signing off I can only advise both author and publisher to be ready to update this volume when it reprints to include the reinstated Loughborough main-line bridge!

LEICESTER CENTRAL: The Great Central Railway was subsumed within the LNER at the 1923 Grouping and it remained in 'Eastern' hands at nationalisation in 1948. Sadly, the late 1950s saw the transfer of the route to Marylebone to Midland Region hands and, shortly after, the withdrawal of 'The South Yorkshireman' prestige train, leading to the removal of glorious sights such as No 60102 *Sir Frederick Banbury* **making a storming exit from Leicester Central station on 14 August 1950, on its way to London.** *Alec Ford, MJS collection*

Introduction

I have produced many 'Past & Present' books and all have given me great pleasure, but this particular volume has an added spice for me, knowing, as I have, the Great Central Railway for nigh on 60 years. Successfully passing the eleven-plus exams at Thurmaston Junior School, I arrived at Loughborough College School in September 1954, travelling, as part of my journey from home in Thurmaston, by train from Syston station. In that first year I was intrigued to witness several of my fellow students assiduously noting and collecting locomotive numbers during our rail journeys, so much so that I determined to play my part in the trainspotting fraternity. Thus, at the beginning of the new school academic year in September 1955 the first numbers garnered at Loughborough Midland station were entered into a newly acquired exercise book. I was quickly to notice that on the line that crossed the Midland by a bridge at the southern end of Loughborough station the loco numbers, by and large, began with a '6' rather than a '4', as on the Midland. Enquiring as to their provenance, my love affair with the GCR was born.

The main protagonists in the drama contained within these pages are the steam motive power and the inherent infrastructure bequeathed to us by the engineers from 1899, and I have always felt great satisfaction that fortune granted me the opportunity of viewing the magnificent 'A3s' – not least No 60102 *Sir Frederick Banbury*, one of my all-time favourites – on the southbound 'South Yorkshireman' expresses. Sadly, the GC, far-sightedly constructed to the more

generous 'Berne Gauge', the continental standard, was to fall foul of political decisions and bias following transfer of the route to the Midland Region of British Railways in the late 1950s. There was an unseemly haste to downgrade, divert and destroy over the final decade to 1969. Happily, a disparate collection of individuals and organisations have seen, over time, to the salvation and restoration of the line between south Nottingham and north Leicester, and it is with real delight and honour that I present this collection of comparative views.

Being Leicester born and bred I knew much about the route, but I have also learned more from the research, visits and preparation for this volume. It is also with a heightened sense of excitement that, at the time of writing, there has been an announcement that the long-lamented 'gap' over the Midland at Loughborough is to be plugged and that the line will again be complete between the two cities.

Many of us appreciate the appeal and romance of the whole route into Marylebone, and I am pleased to have been able to display some of this in just a relatively short stretch. I hope readers will enjoy this present look at the route and that it will kindle a desire to visit the existing remains, support the present and savour the tantalising prospect of travelling over the new bridge in just a few years' time. Volunteers are always welcomed on private railways, as is their monetary support. With shed loads of both, the 'reunification' will come sooner rather than later!

NOTTINGHAM VICTORIA: Your author has fond memories of taking his lunches in the restaurant at Leicester Central station on many occasions in the very early 1960s, where the days of *Brief Encounter* lived on, complete with monogrammed cutlery and china. This was the scene still on offer at Nottingham Victoria on the last day of through trains to and from Marylebone, 3 September 1966! We cannot read the tariff board, but tea, alcohol, hot Bovril and Kia-Ora are all certainly on offer. *S. B. Lee/Colour-Rail collection*

ANNESLEY SHED: Situated in the mid-west of Nottinghamshire, south of Hollinwell & Annesley station, Annesley shed was one of two that supplied traction for the GCR route to the south of Nottingham. Opened in 1898, to service the new Great Central line, it was a predominantly freight depot, with a wide variety of locomotives at its disposal over the years. On 24 July 1955 'Austerity' class leader No 90000, wearing the 38A shedplate from nearby Colwick shed, stands in company with sister No 90052 and 'B1' No 61201. *Brian Morrison*

After transfer to BR(LMR) in 1958, the pedigree of locos on shed became increasingly ex-LMS. On 13 November 1965 No 45292 seems to be losing a fair proportion of its available steam as it prepares to leave for the next duty. Predominantly a West Coast Main Line (WCML) engine for its BR life, it was never actually officially allocated to the GCR route but was a frequent performer during the later days of the line and, indeed, worked the last northbound passenger turn on 3 September 1966. *Bryan Hicks*

Above: **COLWICK** was the second shed; actually closer to Nottingham than Annesley, it was built and operated by the GNR. Originally opened in 1876, it was extended and re-roofed on numerous occasions right up to 1960. Standing outside the original four-road shed, Mexborough (36B)-allocated Class 'O4/7' 2-8-0 No 63699 has been coaled and watered and looks in fine style, complete with the early 'cycling lion' BR logo on the tender, ready to return home with a freight working on 24 July 1955. *Brian Morrison*

Below: The shed was closed to steam on 12 December 1966 and to diesels on 13 April 1970, and was summarily demolished the following year. On shed in May 1960, No 68927 also looks smart in the sunshine, this time with the later 'ferret and dartboard' BR logo. Despite its smart outward appearance, the elderly ex-GNR No 228 was to survive only a further 12 months before withdrawal. *MJS collection*

NOTTINGHAM VICTORIA, the GCR station in Nottingham, was much loved by enthusiasts and railway historians but, with the platforms below ground level, was not so well thought of by its travelling clientele. This undated view displays its wonderful clock tower at street level, together with its porte-cochère, standing adjacent to the Victoria Hotel, built by the GCR to cater for its more wealthy customers. The main building, in glorious Victorian splendour, used the best quality red brick and Darley Dale stone, and was officially opened on 24 May 1900, to coincide with Queen Victoria's birthday.

Closed by BR on 4 September 1967, the station building was entirely demolished (except for the clock tower) and the Victoria Centre shopping precinct built on the site, thankfully incorporating the clock tower into the main entrance on Milton Street. The Hilton Hotel group now occupies the old hotel site and the architecture of this building helps to offset the drab and uninspiring concrete monstrosity that now dominates the scene. Note that the modern view, on 30 April 2013, was taken from street level, as the former vantage point no longer exists. *Colour-Rail collection/Roger Bacon*

NOTTINGHAM VICTORIA: Down in the 'hole' we are still in **LNER** days, as No 4393 of Colwick shed draws into Victoria station with a local from the north on 8 May 1946. Later to become No 2188 under the LNER 1946 renumbering scheme, and subsequently 62188 at nationalisation in 1948, the locomotive was withdrawn in October 1949. The signal box name, 'Nottingham Vic Nth', was later to change. Note the myriad of lines emanating from the tunnel (hidden from sight) underneath the short rows of houses.

The view without the rails, trains and signal box on 23 May 1974 not only looks denuded but also more resembles a modeller's layout than a full-sized, standard gauge station site! The tunnel, especially, looks incongruously small for its purpose, and no evidence remains of there ever having been a railway here. *H. C. Casserley/MJS collection*

NOTTINGHAM VICTORIA: Also seen from the north end of the station, 'K3' No 61826 glides into Victoria station with a local passenger service from Sheffield Victoria around 1961. A long-time servant of the GCR lines around Nottinghamshire from nationalisation, it had spent a little over 18 months at Norwich shed between 1958 and 1960 before returning to Staveley (GC) shed, then Colwick. Withdrawal was from the latter in October 1962.

Some five years earlier, Doncaster (36A)-allocated No 61036 *Ralph Assheton* is seen in September 1956 from the platform closer to the centre of the Victoria complex at the head of a rake of 'blood and custard' coaches, possibly forming a York-Bournemouth turn. Coincidentally, this 'B1' was withdrawn at exactly the same time as the 'K3' above! Note the proliferation of red paint in this colourful view. *MJS collection/ Colour-rail collection*

NOTTINGHAM VICTORIA: These three views at the south end are looking north into the body of the station. On 12 July 1947 we see a 'sister' of the 'D2' entering Victoria on page 12, this time wearing its relatively new, 1946-allocated number 2194. Previously LNER No 3041, it became 62194 at nationalisation in 1948, but only survived until August 1949. The view contains so much of the paraphernalia of days of yore on the railways, both on and off the platform, and also shows the wear and tear of the architecture from the war years. The White Hart Inn proudly announces itself and a nearby building prominently advertises 'Digger' tobacco.

Fourteen years later, on 22 July 1961, the BR(LMR) take-over is in full swing, with Stanier No 42556 of Leicester (Central) shed waiting for the 'off' to head south with a local train to its home location. The turntable is still in use on the right, with a 'B1' on board flying the Eastern flag. The White Hart sign is now not so prominent; and the station canopy has had some refurbishment. The main roof, however, still looks in need of attention.

Another example of the 'Midland' is seen here in the form of 'Royal Scot' No 46165 *The Ranger (12th London Regt.)*, certainly not a type of motive power that would have been seen in this locale a decade earlier. With a few moments before departure for Marylebone, on 13 June 1964, the fireman shares pleasantries with a group of youthful enthusiasts. Less than three years from closure, the station infrastructure is beginning to look decidedly world-weary.

All H. C. Casserley

NOTTINGHAM VICTORIA: In the last year of Eastern Region control the station is a hive of activity, despite the UK still struggling to recover from the vagaries of war, money still being in relatively short supply and the gradually increasing influence of road traffic. No 61369 prepares to continue south with the prestigious 'South Yorkshireman' express on 11 June 1957, while two 'J6' 0-6-0s and an 'A3' 4-6-2 occupy the other platforms. Note the young child in harness, in the father's strong hand, and his belted mac of the period. A couple of spotters admire the express locomotive. *A. G. Cramp/Colour-Rail collection*

Inside the massive train shed at Victoria all is quiet as a very clean-looking No 67741 runs through the middle road between duties and perhaps acting as station pilot. The framing of the ex-GCR lower-quadrant signals and 'Way Out' notice add to the interest on 20 October 1961, together with the trackside disc shunting signals, the large 'Waiting Rooms' sign and the suspended tannoy loudspeaker. *Hugh Ballantyne*

A sign of the times on 12 October 1962 when, in addition to the 'Midland' influence, dieselisation was making inroads into the long-distance trains operating over the GCR. On the left, No D6753, then just a month old and allocated to Darnall shed, Sheffield (41A), has the road to restart its York-Bournemouth journey, while to its right Annesley-based No 92011 is northbound with a freight. *B. W. L. Brooksbank, Initial Photographics collection*

NOTTINGHAM VICTORIA: During its last years the GCR was to see an influx of some glamorous locomotives, displaced from the WCML by the ongoing electrification. Under Victoria's cavernous roof at 8.43pm on an unidentified day in October 1965, the atmospheric view is heightened by the artificial light and a slow shutter speed, graphically evidencing the blowing-off by No 70054, now sadly without its *Dornoch Firth* nameplates. Still nominally allocated to Crewe South (5B) shed at this date, it was shipped north to Carlisle within three months, from where it was withdrawn in December 1966. *Colour-Rail collection*

NOTTINGHAM VICTORIA: We are now just three weeks from the end of through trains to London from Victoria, as No 44984 is about to begin its journey to Marylebone on 14 August 1966. With a skein of coal looped on the platform, the ancient brazier by the water column and the careworn canopy, the station mirrors the rather unkempt condition of the 'Black 5'. Tracks have been lifted in the bay platforms and the path to the turntable is devoid of either motive power or stock that would have been the case in previous times. A solitary spotter has very little to attract his attention! *Alan Donaldson*

One year on and the station is looking decidedly sad on 17 August 1967, with through tracks now lifted, the platform bare apart from discarded barriers and seating, and the delightful lower-quadrant signals having nothing to control. The only tracks now are those made by recovery road vehicles! *Syd Hancock*

NOTTINGHAM VICTORIA: Many transformations are captured by happenstance, as is the case here. On 7 August 1965 the sun shines brightly on the station and No 45299 as it waits to start its journey south to Marylebone. Carriages stand in other platforms awaiting business, the platforms are clean and tidy for the most part, and a photographer prepares the snap the attractively lit train. The architecture and station furniture are still something to enjoy and life lingers on...

...but not for ever! Almost exactly three years later, and very close to the same vantage point, the vista is dramatically altered. The **DMU** that has brought the **SLS** (Midland Area) 'Farewell to **GN** Branch Lines in Derbyshire & Nottinghamshire' rail tour to the station on 4 May 1968 stands isolated in the mid-afternoon, as its participants wander around the site, capturing their last visions of the desecration. Starting from Birmingham New Street at 1020, the journey via Burton-on-Trent, Derby Friargate and Bulwell Common saw arrival at Victoria around 1515 ... but it was not due to stop! *MJS collection/J. M. Tolson, Frank Hornby collection*

NOTTINGHAM ARKWRIGHT STREET station was situated 1 mile south of Nottingham Victoria, perched on a viaduct on the southern approach to the city, high above the surrounding streets of the Meadows. It was one of only two original intermediate stations on the line, as opposed to Halts, to be constructed other than as an island formation. The pastoral name for the area is reflected in the station running-in board, inviting fans to alight here for Trent Bridge and cricket. On an unknown date in the 1950s No 61041 heads south with a Sheffield-Marylebone turn. *Henry Priestley, Milepost 92½, railphotolibrary.com*

Although it is not obvious from the earlier view above, the two wooden platforms were cantilevered out from the double-track viaduct. This view from 2 February 1974 gives some indication of the climb up the steps faced by would-be passengers. Opened on 15 March 1899, Arkwright Street closed initially on 4 March 1963, together with other wayside stations along the line, but was reinstated from 4 September 1967 to act as the northern terminus of the truncated GCR operated from Rugby by DMUs following the closure of nearby Victoria. The last train ran on Saturday 3 May 1969, with final closure on the following Monday. Demolition came in 1975, after which the area was totally redeveloped. *Robin Leleux*

WILFORD: Gresley's 'B17' 4-6-0s were not common visitors to the GCR, usually only seen on special occasions, but in 1950 No 61662 *Manchester United* was one of four allocated to Colwick shed. On 11 October 1951 the 4-6-0 and 'B1' No 61368 provide powerful and slightly unusual power as they rush south near Wilford with a Manchester-Leicester express. One month later the 'Footballer' left the area to undertake duties from Stratford (London) shed.

Fifteen years later another unusual visitor steams south over the River Trent and past the Brick Yard sidings at Wilford. On the last day of the GCR main line as a through route to London, 3 September 1966, No 35030 *Elder Dempster Lines* heads the return LCGB London-Sheffield 'Great Central Rail Tour' at approximately 6.50pm; it has regained the reins between Nottingham and Marylebone, having arrived in the city earlier in the day with the train from Waterloo. *J. P. Wilson, Peter Treloar collection/ Dorothy Hicks*

RUDDINGTON was a typical GCR 'London Extension' island platform, accessed from a road overbridge. Opened in 1899, together with Arkwright Street already seen, the station architecture and platform furniture are virtually identical to its 'sisters' further south, such as Quorn & Woodhouse, Rothley and Belgrave & Birstall. This view, during a quiet period on 3 June 1957, is looking south towards Loughborough from under the aforementioned road, with station and track formation all neat and tidy.

Hardly recognisable as the same location, the platforms are still in situ, visible in the bottom right-hand corner. The overbridge has been rebuilt, hence the different archway effect, and there has been substantial housing development on the erstwhile railway land to the east of the station site. At the time of this visit, on 19 April 2013, the burgeoning Nottingham Tramway was very close to the north (behind the camera), and the GCR(N) preservationists around a quarter of a mile south. The potential would be substantial if the old station site could be reached and used by both. *Richard Casserley/MJS*

RUDDINGTON: Over the years, from around 1920, this photographer travelled widely, by rail and/or car, to capture as much of the UK's railway scene as possible. He accumulated an impressive array of images, many depicting stations, and a healthy percentage were snapped from passing trains. Such was the case here, as he looks back from a southbound train at Ruddington to provide another aspect of the GCR layout and architecture. The sign on the factory wall on the left seems to be 'Robert Baker & Sons Ltd' somewhat inexpertly painted over a previous incarnation.

The modern view from 19 April 2013 is slightly closer to the northern end of the station, dictated by the prolific growth of bushes and trees over the years that would have rendered a strict comparison meaningless. The redesign of the road bridge, on either side of the bricked-up station entrance, is clearly seen. The factory has long since disappeared from the area on the left.
H. C. Casserley/MJS

RUDDINGTON: During the last few years of the GCR as a main line, the available motive power was not to receive the TLC that was once commonplace, with the result that locomotives looked ever more careworn. From this view of No 44984, accelerating away from Ruddington station in May 1966 and passing under the 'Fifty Steps' bridge with a Nottingham-Marylebone express, it is obviously many moons since it had received attention from even an oily rag! The fireman casually views the photographer as, from the leading coach, enthusiasts appear to be recording the sounds of their journey. Note the new housing appearing to the right.

Happily the bridge is still in situ and has even received a goodly lick of paint in recent times, looking decidedly smarter than in 1966. The line here forms the northern extent of Great Central Railway (Nottingham) operations, and on 13 April 2013 'Austerity' saddle tank No 56 has run past the signals on the headshunt and is now returning to the nearby terminus and museum complex in the former Ministry of Defence site east of the line. There are now many more houses on the far side of the hedge to the right. *Colour-Rail collection/MJS*

RUSHCLIFFE HALT sat adjacent to the British Plaster Board Ltd (later British Gypsum) Hotchley Hill Works and was accessed from the Gotham-East Leake road. Only a mile or so north of the latter location, the halt (behind the camera) was initially opened in 1911 to serve the nearby Rushcliffe Golf Club. It was later joined by sidings into the gypsum works immediately to the north. Passenger services ended in 1963, but freight to the works continued until the early 1980s, then recommenced from 2000, via a link from the Midland Main Line at Loughborough. On 16 June 1964 a typically grimy No 92095 powers another famed 'Windcutter' freight southwards on the approach to the halt, with the gypsum works to the right.

Happily, when seen on 13 April 2013 the basic station and track layout are largely unchanged and even the colour light standard is still in place, although not in use. The British Gypsum Head Office, on the right, has been much enlarged over the years and now encompasses all of the company's main facilities, including the Technical Academy, a training facility opened in 1990. No 56 propels its three-coach train from the Rushcliffe Halt stop forming the 1349 Loughborough-Ruddington duty. *Syd Hancock/MJS*

RUSHCLIFFE HALT: A view from the roadway above the halt provides a wider perspective of the station and its surroundings. On 29 June 1962 No 64818 gingerly pushes its varied consist into the sidings as the 1.07pm Queens Walk-Hotchley Hill roster at precisely 2.19pm. Allocated to Ardsley shed in the Leeds area just a week previously, it would be interesting to establish how and why it was working this local freight so far south.

The dramatic expansion over the half century since the earlier view is obvious in this aspect from 13 April 2013. Though unprepossessing at first glance, this unremarkable halt is the last of the few remaining twin-platform structures on the GCR south of Nottingham. The GCR(N) preservationists have done a good job in making the facility look so clean and presentable.
David Holmes/MJS

RUSHCLIFFE HALT: Back on the platform, we face south to witness No 44825 rushing through non-stop on 18 June 1966 with the 2.38pm Marylebone-Nottingham Victoria semi-fast. Note that the closure of the halt to passengers in 1963 is evidenced by the blanking off of the footbridge on the far platform. Again, No 44825 is not in the smartest condition. At this date it was shedded at Annesley, for GCR duties, but had spent most of its BR time on the Midland Main Line, predominantly at Nottingham, Derby and Cricklewood. Subsequent to the end of steam on the GCR, it moved north to Carlisle, from where its end came on 7 October 1967.

On normal working days the GCR(N) trains occupy just the old up line, as seen here on 13 April 2013, as No 56 propels its carriages towards the camera as the 1149 Loughborough-Ruddington service. The erstwhile footbridge has disappeared, leaving access on this side from the roadway, and a roundabout trip to ground level close to the works for boarding trains on the far side. *Mike Mitchell, MJS collection/ MJS*

EAST LEAKE was the first major station south of Ruddington and was again an island platform. It boasted, at its height, a full panoply of facilities, both passenger and freight, with three sidings under its jurisdiction, including that at Hotchley Hill. It closed to passengers in 1963 together with the other wayside stations on the line, but remained open for freight after the end of through services to and from Marylebone; the end finally came on 5 May 1969, when the whole line was finally closed. New in April 1950, No 61367 is seen restarting its northbound train on 29 April 1956, when shedded at Colwick, with a solitary spotter in attendance.

Fifty-seven years later, on 13 April 2013, the platforms are in situ but no longer in use, despite rails running alongside on the left of this view, over which both **GCR(N)** and gypsum trains travel. Lack of local parking and the filling-in of the previous midway entrance from the road below have dictated that there are no plans in the foreseeable future to reinstate this facility. This view is slightly closer to the ramp of the platform, as the verdant growth behind the camera precluded a meaningful exact present-day equivalent. *Milepost 92½, railphotolibrary.com/MJS*

EAST LEAKE: On the platform and turning round to face north, we see **No 61846** at precisely 6.07pm on 6 June 1962 heading south with the 5.25pm Annesley-Woodford Halse mixed freight. The fireman is taking a breather, despite the train climbing the 1 in 264 gradient through the station. Note the relatively open vista to the right. Allocated to Hull (Dairycoates) shed at this date, the engine, on this wholly GCR run, is far away from its home. It was withdrawn just seven months later.

The comparative view shows change both on and off the railway. No 56 passes over the roadway on 13 April 2013, some 10 minutes late with the 1100 Ruddington-Loughborough GCR(N) train. The platforms are now devoid of buildings, but the view to the right shows the arrival of housing that has contributed to the decision not to reopen the station. *David Holmes/MJS*

EAST LEAKE:
Immediately south of the station the railway runs into a cutting that stretches for some distance, the gradient hardening for some of it to 1 in 176. The sun is shining but dark clouds are gathering in June 1966 as No 45426 heads one of the remaining Nottingham-Rugby semi-fasts away from the station. The typical GCR architecture is clear from this view, as is the careworn appearance of the 'Black 5' in these latter days.

The cutting sides on 13 April 2013 are now not as pristine as of yore and the brambles are a trap for the unwary! Old track panels, complete with scatterings of spent ballast, sit alongside the running line that sees the occasional gypsum train disturbing the sylvan setting. Interestingly, the colour light signal, just visible to the left of the station site in the earlier view, is still in situ, hidden among the undergrowth on the left, but now without spectacle plate or filaments! *Colour-Rail collection/ MJS*

BARNSTON TUNNEL: Roughly a mile south of East Leake station, the 110-yard-long Barnston Tunnel stood at the summit of the line between Nottingham Victoria and Loughborough Central, with much of the approach from north and south at 1 in 176. Bursting forth from the northern portal on a hazy but bright 14 October 1962, at precisely 12.27pm, No 61438 is in fine form on the last leg of its part in the LCGB 'Midland Limited Rail Tour' from Marylebone to Nottingham. Using four further locomotives, the tour made a convoluted trip around the Midlands area before returning to London St Pancras.

Seen from the same location, but this time across the tracks, No 6906 *Chicheley Hall* heads the Saturdays-only Poole-Leeds/Bradford express on 22 August 1964. Unlike

No 61438 above, the fireman of the 'Hall' is taking it easy with his charge down the ruling gradient and using the opportunity to check on the position of the photographer. In 1964 Western Region locos worked the train as far north as Nottingham, where they were replaced by 'Jubilee' 4-6-0s based at Farnley Junction, unlike the previous year, when the 'Jubilees' were on the train as far as Leicester. From the following year the train worked to and from Nottingham via the Midland line. *David Holmes/Syd Hancock*

BARNSTON TUNNEL: Moving to the southern exit from Barnston Tunnel, beneath the Hathern-Wymeswold road 3 miles north of Loughborough, No 44690 is obviously being worked hard, despite the falling gradient, on the final part of its journey as the 1.23pm Skegness-Leicester holiday working on 24 August 1963. Departing from Leicester Central shed and the GCR just three months later, the 'Black 5' finally ended up in the North West and was one of the last steam locos to survive to the end of steam in 1968. *Mike Mitchell, MJS collection*

Below: **Enjoying the 2 miles of 1 in 176 falling gradient, No 45292 is virtually coasting as it sweeps around the graceful curve away from the tunnel on the approach to Stanford-on-Soar as the 5.15pm Nottingham Victoria-Marylebone semi-fast on 31 July 1965. The late-afternoon sunshine nicely picks out the train and its delightfully rural surroundings. A long-term servant of the WCML, the 'Black 5' was on loan to the GCR for much of the last two years of the through route's existence, before returning west and withdrawal in December 1967.** *Mike Mitchell, MJS collection*

STANFORD-ON-SOAR: In the later years of the GCR route most of the motive power was of LMS extraction, and slightly more glamorous motive power arrived, ousted from the WCML by electrification. Just yards from the views on the previous page, No 46122 *Royal Ulster Rifleman* is one such, heading south with another Nottingham Victoria-Marylebone semi-fast on 16 May 1964. Having worked from Annesley shed since December 1962, it returned home to Carlisle five months after this view, from where it was summarily withdrawn. *Syd Hancock*

Turning to look south, No 45708 *Resolution* approaches Fox Hill at Stanford with a northbound working in 1963. Judging by the loco's allocation to Farnley Junction shed in Leeds, it is probably another summer Saturday inter-regional holiday train (see the comments on page 30). New in 1936, the loco's end came in March 1964, another wasteful abandonment of a valuable railway asset. *Syd Hancock*

STANFORD VIADUCT: On the approach to Loughborough Central from the north, the GCR crossed the River Soar by a graceful multi-arched viaduct, supported by sturdy brick pillars, two of which stood within the river itself. Looking magnificent as it crosses this edifice on 28 July 1955, No 60102 *Sir Frederick Banbury* handles this short level stretch with ease at the head of the 3.20pm Marylebone-Manchester London Road express, which includes a Restaurant Car. A long-term resident of 38C (Leicester Central) shed until September 1957, your author was treated to sights of it on the southbound 'South Yorkshireman' express in 1955/56 during brief trips to the station in lunch breaks from Loughborough College School!

Happily, despite the route closing in 1969, the presence of the gypsum traffic saved the line over the viaduct, to the extent that GCR(N) trains now run to this point from Ruddington, and at the time of writing there is the very real prospect of the two halves of the GCR being reunited in the foreseeable future. On 6 May 2013 Class 47 No 47292 stands in for two failed steam engines with a return working from Loughborough to the northern terminus. *G. D. King/David Richards*

LOUGHBOROUGH MIDLAND station was where your author started trainspotting and developed his love of railways. Views like this greeted him and his compatriots as they waited for their local train home after school, which would pull into the Midland station after 'The Thames-Clyde Express' had roared through! On a dull day in December 1949 No 1248, still in its LNER garb two years after nationalisation, heads north across the Midland Main Line with an unfitted freight. Note the large advert for Loughborough College, lauding its engineering prowess; the gas lamp and starter signal at the end of the platform; and the siding to the right of the main line. The college is now much better known for its sporting facilities, and the siding disappeared during the next decade.

No 222014 approaches Loughborough Midland station on 2 July 2011 forming the 1425 East Midlands Trains service from St Pancras to Sheffield. The central pillar of the former GCR overbridge was where the green colour light now stands, and the left-hand abutment against the old embankment is to the extreme left; the supporting pillar was between the slow lines, roughly in line with the right-hand red colour light on the gantry, and the right-hand pillar was out of shot to the right. With the planned reinstatement of a bridge by the GCR and Network Rail, this view will again change. *MJS collection/MJS*

LOUGHBOROUGH CENTRAL station was much closer to the centre of the town than its Midland neighbour, but sadly the GCR was not as well blessed by either passenger trains or actual travellers. Its saving grace was the large amount of freight handled, both local and long-distance. With evidence of the removal of tracks through the station and to the warehouse, No 44941 restarts from the Loughborough call with the 5.15pm Marylebone-Nottingham Victoria three-coach semi-fast in August 1966. The large Morris Cranes factory is to the left.

Over the three decades since the fledgling **GCR** preservationists inherited the site, the vista has been considerably improved, with tracks relaid and much (diesel) stock on view, as seen from the signal box on 10 March 2006. Note how the railway's neighbours on the left have populated the area with fresh building. *Colour-Rail collection/MJS*

LOUGHBOROUGH CENTRAL: We have already seen evidence of Loughborough College advertising, alongside the Midland Main Line, but the sign here is more blatant, despite the Central station being as far away from the actual College as the Midland. It is dubious how many extra travellers used this route to reach the learned establishment. This view from the 1930s epitomises the often very peaceful nature of the GCR, even in those busy pre-war days. Note the rather surprising Romney, Hythe & Dymchurch Railway notice board, plugging Dungeness!

As part of filming for a forthcoming feature film, *Cemetery Junction*, written and directed by Ricky Gervais and Stephen Merchant, Loughborough Central station was 'converted' to become the eponymous location. The GCR was closed for the week to 26 June 2009 for the filming to take place, but reversion to normality was still in hand when seen on the following day, Saturday 27th. Note the transformation of the northern end of the station building – looking incredibly realistic, even on the ground – and the renamed running-in board! *MJS collection/MJS*

LOUGHBOROUGH CENTRAL: Although Brush Engineering's massive Falcon Works was adjacent to the Midland station in Loughborough, the GCR was used on occasion to test the new Type 2 diesels being built there. With the number of timetabled services far fewer than on the Midland, there was much less chance of disruption during testing periods. On 4 October 1961 No D5637 is undergoing unidentified tests, 15 months after it appeared as new from Brush. Initially allocated to 30A (Stratford) shed, it remained an ER loco for many years and has had many different persona following tweaking and 'rebuilds'. As No 31465 it was still extant at the time of writing.

In the same position on 2 July 2011, the much newer D5830 stands at rest at the end of its journey as the 1345 Leicester North-Loughborough Central service. With surroundings on either side of the line little changed over the years, the vista is one of less openness and freedom. Becoming No 31297 under the TOPS renumbering in May 1974, this loco has also had different identities. Withdrawn from squadron service at Toton depot on 19 February 1998, it now enjoys retirement on the GCR, painted in one of the experimental BR colour schemes. *MJS collection/MJS*

LOUGHBOROUGH CENTRAL: On what looks to be a very cold and overcast winter's day, the lighting does no favours for the state of the 'Black 5' on this duty. On 5 January 1965 No 45190 accelerates away from Loughborough Central station with an unidentified Nottingham-Rugby semi-fast, as the fireman looks back along his three-coach train. It is to be hoped that the steam heating was working fully in the carriages! A Shrewsbury shed veteran for much of its BR life, No 45190 transferred to Annesley in October 1964, following the closure of the West Midlands shed. It ended its life, in May 1968, in the Manchester area.

Another bitterly cold and snowy day sees **LNER No 4498** *Sir Nigel Gresley* (aka BR No 60007), magnificent in its garter blue livery, making an explosive exit from the station almost exactly 28 years later, on 28 December 1993, with the 1300 service to Leicester North during a post-Christmas Gala. New in 1937, the engine is one of six of the class to escape the cutter's torch following its withdrawal in 1966. *MJS collection/MJS*

WOODTHORPE: On its exit from Loughborough the GCR line passes under the A6 'London-Carlisle' trunk road. On 15 February 1952 No 61225 proudly displays 'The South Yorkshireman' headboard as it bursts from underneath the bridge with the early afternoon express southbound for Marylebone. More normally an 'A3' roster, this was undoubtedly a prestigious outing for the more humble 'B1'.

A few yards further south No 70013 *Oliver Cromwell* also wears the celebrity headboard, but this time in preservation. The engine looks in truly fine fettle as it hauls the 1500 Loughborough Central-Leicester North train on 5 May 2008. Note the gricers savouring their menu of smoke and speed! *Bryan Jennings, MJS collection/MJS*

WOODTHORPE: We are now on the Leicester side of the narrow road bridge from which *Oliver Cromwell* was captured on the previous page, and No 92091 is obviously working hard as it heads south with one the GCR's famed 'Windcutter' freight trains. In March 1965, when the loco was allocated to Annesley shed, it is obviously some time since it received the attentions of an oily rag! It served the GCR route well between March 1957 and July 1965, after which it moved to Birkenhead for a further two years of life.
N. F. Ingram, Colour-Rail collection

This is the same vantage point but now looking south, as No 92069 has a slightly easier task as it speeds down the 1 in 176 gradient from Quorn & Woodhouse on 13 June 1964, with a rake of oil tanks in tow. New to Doncaster (36A) shed in January 1956, its GCR tenure and destination were almost identical to No 92091 above, except that its departure to Birkenhead came in May 1965. Note the overall neatness both on and off the railway. *Mike Mitchell, MJS collection*

QUORN & WOODHOUSE: The GCR route was renowned for its freight handling, and the range of traffic was wide and varied. A good example of variety is seen in this view of No 63713, climbing the gradient to Quorn on 19 June 1950 with a veritable motley collection of goods and produce. Emerging from Robert Stephenson & Co, for the Government's Railway Operating Division (ROD) to assist with First World War railway needs, it was not to become an LNER loco until November 1927. In this view it seems to be showing signs of age, but it lasted a further 12 years until withdrawal from Gorton shed in September 1962.

As can be seen, the northern approach to Quorn & Woodhouse station has been recreated to almost its former basic track layout in the post-closure restoration. Just a little of the climb can

be judged from this view of the track looking towards Loughborough, as No 45305 begins to slow for the station stop on 11 August 2004, with the 1030 Loughborough Central-Leicester North service, masquerading as 'The Master Cutler', one of the late-lamented named trains of the former GCR route. *Bryan Jennings, MJS collection/MJS*

QUORN & WOODHOUSE: Down on the ground, yet another grimy 'Black 5' is on hand on Friday 26 August 1966, just eight days from closure. Someone has attempted some improvement in its status by chalking an unofficial nameplate on the side of No 45289's boiler but, despite the healthy accommodation provided by seven coaches on this Nottingham Victoria-Marylebone service, it is nothing more than humdrum this late in the GCR's history. The loco was much travelled during its BR life and had a mere three months left before withdrawal.

At close to the same point 33 years later, on 16 June 1999, the preservationists have made great strides in recreating the main-line experience, even to providing a 9F to assist with passenger duties. No 92212, in the hands of then GCR Director Nigel Harris as fireman, approaches Quorn & Woodhouse with the 1315 Loughborough Central-Leicester North service, passing an engineering possession for Unimog testing by Messrs Amey – hence the buckling of the untamped rails. *Syd Hancock/MJS*

QUORN & WOODHOUSE: Looking south from the roadway that crosses the line here, No 44858 drifts into the station with just five coaches, met by bright late-afternoon summer sunshine, forming another Marylebone-Nottingham Victoria turn. Note how open the whole site appears, not least due to the lifting of the erstwhile siding alongside the train, and the invitation on the ground 'HOT DOG, DO HAVE ONE'! Another widely travelled engine, its stay at Annesley, officially from the day after this photograph, was a mere three months before it sampled pastures new around Liverpool.

While the last days of the GCR as a main line saw a very limited number of different locomotives, one of the pleasures of the preserved regime is the presence of visiting types and identities. On Bank Holiday Monday, 6 May 2013, one of the rarer beasts pauses at Quorn with a returning service to Loughborough from Leicester North. Built at Crewe Works in 1888 to Webb's design, the 'Coal Tank' is here in its LNWR guise as No 1054. Normally housed at the Keighley & Worth Valley Railway, and formerly BR No 58926, it travelled to the Severn Valley Railway in 2012 for a short visit as LMS No 7799. *Syd Hancock/David Richards*

KINCHLEY LANE: On the northern approach to Swithland Reservoir, the railway runs under Kinchley Lane, a meandering country lane joining two near parallel roads north of Swithland and Rothley. Passing a Distant signal on the down line, No 61369 climbs the 1 in 264 gradient as it prepares to pass under the road with an afternoon Manchester London Road-Marylebone express on 6 June 1951. Note the high positioning of the smokebox numberplate.

Looking for all the world like a routine service in BR days in the North West, with the 'Manchester Vic via Moston' destination blind, GCR's two-car DMU (E50321 leading) approaches Kinchley Lane on Saturday 13 April 2013 forming the 0940 Loughborough Central-Leicester North service, first train of the day. The semaphore has disappeared and the embankment has had a recent haircut.
Bryan Jennings, MJS collection/MJS

ROTHLEY:
Another 'Black
5', with seven
carriages behind,
is lit by bright late-
afternoon sunshine
as it travels from
Nottingham
Victoria to
Marylebone. On 28
May 1966 No 45464
liberally pollutes
the atmosphere
as it approaches
Rothley station,
through which it
will steam without
stopping, as the
station had closed
from 4 March 1963.
A Scottish loco for
many years, it was
based at Perth until
March 1957, when
it moved south to
Blackpool, then the
East Midlands from
May 1963.

More than three decades later, another 'Black 5' is captured
at the same spot, but now in preservation. Back after overhaul,
No 44767, adorned with a 'Belfast Boat Express' headboard,
approaches Rothley station on Saturday 30 January 2010 with the
1040 Loughborough Central-Leicester North service, during the
GCR 'Lostock & Several Smoking Barrels' three-day gala. Note
that the old goods shed has all its windows and door bricked up.
A. Gooch, Colour-Rail collection/MJS

ROTHLEY: In its post-Second World War heyday, the GCR route gave spotters in the centre of the country the opportunity of viewing iconic **LNER** locomotives without having to travel to the East Coast Main Line. Though Rothley station was still open on 22 August 1959, York-based No 60918 roars through non-stop on an express passenger turn, presumably one of the York-Bournemouth inter-regional services. The station and its surroundings are clean and tidy, gas lamps still stand proudly, and one of the adverts extols the benefits of visiting the Home Life Exhibition!

On 20 April 2013 No 46521 reaches the same spot, but the whole ambience is now very different. Happily, the interest and efforts of the restorationists in the early 1970s succeeded in preserving the station architecture, and the coats of paint, the introduction of flower beds and the presence of staff in uniform greatly enhance this 21st-century view as the 1200 Loughborough Central-Leicester North service slows for its stop. *Milepost 92½, railphotolibrary.com/MJS*

FUND-RAISING: One vital element of any venture is funding and cash flow, and private railways are certainly no exception. In the early days of the 'new' GCR, various fundraising events were held, including a sponsored walk from Leicester's Abbey Lane Sidings to Loughborough and back, along the then still extant track. On 20 June 1971 your author (right) pauses for his portrait with companion Peter Simmonds, on the outward trek in this view looking north through the pipe bridge towards Kinchley Lane overbridge.

Later the same day the (now very) weary walkers are on the return journey and are approaching Birstall. Pausing briefly to capture this view near Greengate Lane, evidence of track-lifting is plain to see. *Judi Stretton/MJS*

BIRSTALL: The aforementioned Greengate Lane and its road overbridge are just in view in the distance beyond this southbound train, seen from a now unused farmer's bridge. An anonymous 'Black 5' 4-6-0 heads a Summer Saturdays-only holiday train, returning to Leicester from either Scarborough or Cleethorpes on 27 June 1963. Again the external condition of the motive power leaves a little to be desired as it coasts its ten-coach train down the 1 in 176 gradient.

Hardly recognisable as the same place, the encroachment of the embankment on the right and proliferation of trees and bushes gives a 'corridor' feel, totally lacking the openness of the earlier scene. The line south of Rothley is single-track, and No 46521 hauls a mixed rake behind it as it operates as the 0945 Loughborough Central-Leicester North driver training turn. New from Swindon Works in 1953, this 60-year-old loco now enjoys its retirement at the GCR. *G. D. King/MJS*

GREAT CENTRAL RAILWAY
LOUGHBOROUGH, LEICESTERSHIRE

RE-CREATING THE EXPERIENCE

BIRSTALL: Now on the ground, a few yards further south, a pair of dirty '8F' Class 2-8-0s head south past this upper area of Birstall with an engineer's train on Saturday evening 27 June 1963. The view is taken north of Park Road bridge, looking towards the Fielding Lane footpath crossing. It was unusual to see double-headed '8Fs' on the GCR, even on engineer's trains; possibly one of the locos was being worked south rather than as 'light engine'.

Such has been the proliferation of greenery at this location that the view of the workmen's hut and the line is now hidden from the earlier vantage point, leading to this comparative view being closer to the foot crossing. On 2 June 2013 the GCR DMU set (Nos 50266, 50321 and 51427) forms the 0940 Loughborough Central-Leicester North service, the first train of the day, trying to emulate the 1966-69 Nottingham-Rugby service with the 'false' destination blind. *G. D. King/MJS*

BELGRAVE & BIRSTALL:
The northern end of
Belgrave & Birstall
station was only at its
photographic best in the
early morning, when the
light was from the east.
Taking advantage of a
glorious morning on 31
August 1961, the camera
has captured this delightful
view of No 61206, with a
healthy supply of coal in the
tender, leaving the station
with the 9.30am Leicester
Central-Nottingham
Victoria stopper. The
island platform is through
the archway, noticeboards
adorn the overbridge sides,
and the local golf course
clubhouse is to the right.

Approaching 12 months
later, the sun was absent
as the photographer
snapped No 92012 at the
head of a northbound
empty 'Windcutter' train
on 14 August 1962. New
in June 1954, to March
shed, the 9F became an
Annesley resident in June
1957 and presumably was
still working from that shed
when seen here, although
nominally it had been
transferred to Cardiff ten
months earlier! *G. D. King/Les
Wade, MJS collection*

Opposite bottom left and right: **How the mighty are fallen! Twenty years on from the previous view the rails and hoardings have gone but the station entrance still stands open on 27 December 1982, 13 years after final closure. There are new tracks at ground level, caused by local off-road motor cyclists using it as a racetrack. Judging by the number of cars in the car park (upper right), the golf club is doing good business.**

Compared to the earlier views, the scene is now one of desolation as viewed by a nine-year-old Adam Stretton on 31 May 1986. The tracks have gone and all signs of them obliterated; the station entrance from the road bridge has been bricked up; nature is reclaiming the property; and the view to the golf clubhouse is increasingly constrained. Happily, progress was being made behind the scenes, and tracks returned in 1988 courtesy of the new regime. */MJS (2)*

BELGRAVE & BIRSTALL: We now stand on Station Road looking down to the platform as an unidentified BR Standard 9F 2-10-0 braves the pouring rain with a rake of flat wagons, passing the station signal box on 27 June 1959. The signal rodding, permanent way and station architecture all appear smartly turned out, despite the wet conditions. Belgrave & Birstall station had an additional building not included in the normal 'London Extension' island platform station layout – this is the square building between the ladies' waiting room and the gents toilet. There are several theories as to its use, including a shelter for travelling ticket inspectors while changing trains, but there is no definite information as to its true purpose.

A decade or so later, the second picture shows the view in around 1970. The tracks have not been used for a year or so and are quickly being colonised by grass, but the station buildings are largely intact. It is interesting to see my father captured digging on his allotment, a place where I spent many happy hours in earlier years, spotting during the time the ground was rented and worked by my grandfather! *Milepost 92½, railphotolibrary.com/Paul Anderson, MJS collection*

BELGRAVE & BIRSTALL: Forward to Friday 19 April 2013, and it can be seen how the old Belgrave & Birstall station has morphed into the new Leicester North. 'King' No 6023, renumbered and renamed 6015 *King Richard III* to celebrate the recently discovered remains of the monarch in Leicester, stands at the platform with the 2025 departure for Loughborough Central, a 'King Richard III Society' special dining train. Turned to face north for Michael Portillo the previous weekend, the loco was not in a healthy condition on this day and was failed after this trip. *MJS*

The 'King' seen opposite was indeed a rarity on the GCR, and so was this locomotive. Moved to the line specifically for this special working, No 61665 *Leicester City* recovers from a signal check as it climbs the gradient into Belgrave & Birstall station with the 'City of Leicester Central Holiday Express' on 17 August 1956, bound for Bridlington. Note the football standing proud beneath the nameplate on the splasher, which was painted in the club's blue and white colours. Spending the whole of its BR existence switching between Norwich and Yarmouth (South Town) sheds, its demise came in April 1959, after which one of its nameplates was donated to the football club. *G. D. King*

BELGRAVE & BIRSTALL was, as with the original **GCR** stations already seen, an island affair, with a largely standard layout of buildings and a central entrance from a roadway above. As seen on 8 August 1959 the facilities are well kept and the station has had a new enamel running-in board, following transfer to the **LMR** a year or so earlier. With the pathway on the right running past the allotments, this was the view that your author so enjoyed as a young lad.

No, that is not me on the fence! On a very bright but obviously cold 2 March 1963, No 76052 pulls into the station, greeted by a disappointingly small knot of expectant passengers, considering that this was the last day of stopping services at these intermediate stations. The BR 'Standard 4' 2-6-0 was another rare beast on the line, but was shedded at Woodford Halse at the time, so had probably been appropriated by Leicester shed. *Both Barry Hilton*

BELGRAVE & BIRSTALL: Fourteen months on from the previous view, another **BR** Standard loco, this time **No 73032**, heads south through the station, but this time non-stop as a Nottingham Victoria-Leicester Central semi-fast on 9 May 1964. The driver peers from his cab as his portrait is taken. Having spent spells in Scotland (from new in June 1953) and with BR(WR) in Bristol, this was another widely travelled loco, reaching the GCR in 1960 and leaving two months after this view.

The view from 27 December 1982 again evidences the frequent presence of motor cyclists, with their tracks this time scouring the platform. Grass and bushes are rapidly gaining the upper hand. Unlike the stations at Quorn and Rothley, Belgrave & Birstall was to suffer numerous bouts of vandalism, leading to the need to demolish the whole structure and rethink the layout completely on restoration. *Both MJS*

BELGRAVE & BIRSTALL is seen again when local stopping trains still served it. No 44683 gains momentum on the down gradient as it leaves with another Nottingham Victoria-Leicester Central train on 19 January 1963.

The second view is another from our visit on a mournful 27 December 1982, and again shows the scars from the cycle tyres and the disappearance of the erstwhile signal box, which stood immediately in front of the large tree on the right.

The new arrangement, known as Leicester North and forced upon the preservationists by the past vandalism, is clearly visible in this view from 14 August 1994. Another rare and glamorous locomotive type is the centre of attention, as the National Railway Museum's pride and joy, No 46229 *Duchess of Hamilton*, arrives with the 0930 service from Loughborough Central. Both crew members are obviously aware of their charge's importance! *G. D. King/MJS (2)*

BELGRAVE & BIRSTALL:
Before... The station is closed, but through trains still run and the permanent way is well cared for on 27 June 1965.

During... The station buildings have gone by 30 April 1988, but new track has arrived, presenting a real statement of intent by the new GCR.

And after...! The 1320 Loughborough Central-Leicester North train arrives at its destination on 30 January 2010 behind No 78019, during the GCR 'Lostock & Several Smoking Barrels' three-day gala. *All MJS*

BELGRAVE & BIRSTALL: Turning our view to the south from our perch on the footpath fencing, the stand of tall trees that has been a landmark at Birstall for so many years is the backdrop to No 60878 as it reaches the slightly easier 1 in 300 gradient through the station with a down fitted freight on 31 August 1961.

The mid-1960s were the changeover years for the through workings on the GCR, with new motive power making its appearance. On 5 June 1965 an unidentified EE Type 3 heads past the signal box with 1N83, another Bournemouth-York inter-regional express.

Once more during our visit on 27 December 1982 the slightly soggy trackbed is now temporary resting place for two gypsies and their dogs. The tall trees look somewhat denuded, but still stand defiant. *G. D. King/MJS (2)*

BELGRAVE & BIRSTALL: This magnificent view beautifully portrays the signal box and its lamp hut in an undated view from around 1909, as attractively designed **GCR Class '8B' 'Atlantic'** No 1093 storms up the hill to Belgrave & Birstall with a Marylebone-Manchester London Road express of all-clerestory stock. The loco was one of a batch of 12 of the class built with a slightly higher working pressure, though this was reduced to the 'standard' 180psi before 1923. The lamp hut on the left was to disappear long before the closure of the box.

A few yards closer to Leicester, No 61279 climbs the bank towards the station with a long train of pigeon vans on Saturday evening 27 June 1963. New in March 1948, after nationalisation although ordered by and to a design of the **LNER**, the 'B1' began its life in Lincoln and spent the whole of its existence there or Norwich, Stratford or Doncaster; its end came at Doncaster in October 1963, less than three months after this scene, when it appears to be working so smoothly. Note the tall chimneys of industrial Leicester in the background. *William Bradshaw/MJS collection/G. D. King*

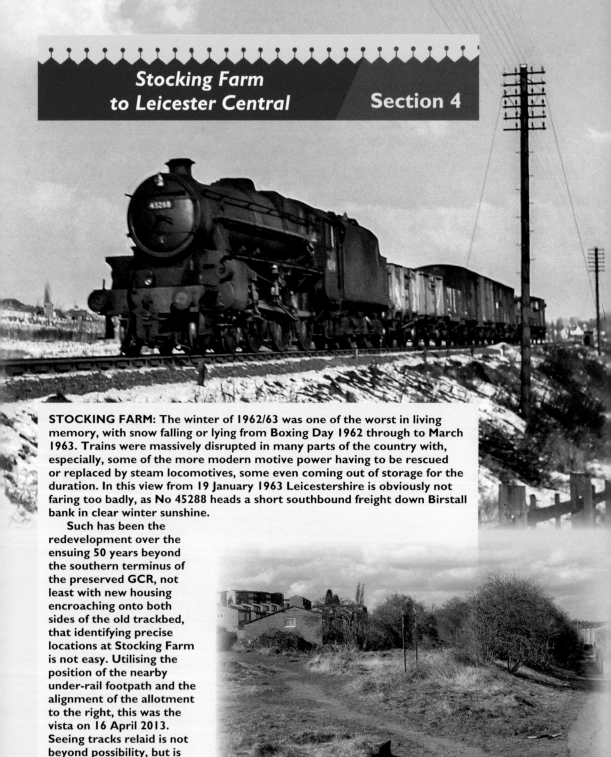

STOCKING FARM: The winter of 1962/63 was one of the worst in living memory, with snow falling or lying from Boxing Day 1962 through to March 1963. Trains were massively disrupted in many parts of the country with, especially, some of the more modern motive power having to be rescued or replaced by steam locomotives, some even coming out of storage for the duration. In this view from 19 January 1963 Leicestershire is obviously not faring too badly, as No 45288 heads a short southbound freight down Birstall bank in clear winter sunshine.

Such has been the redevelopment over the ensuing 50 years beyond the southern terminus of the preserved GCR, not least with new housing encroaching onto both sides of the old trackbed, that identifying precise locations at Stocking Farm is not easy. Utilising the position of the nearby under-rail footpath and the alignment of the allotment to the right, this was the vista on 16 April 2013. Seeing tracks relaid is not beyond possibility, but is highly unlikely. *G. D. King/ MJS*

STOCKING FARM: Crossing the tracks and now looking south towards the city of Leicester, No 61206, with its smokebox number positioned high up, climbs the bank at Stocking Farm with a Marylebone-Nottingham Victoria train on 28 June 1961, consisting of six coaches and a goods van.

Four years later the motive power is both more powerful and, until very recently, a stranger to the GCR route. In September 1965, ousted from the WCML duties by diesels and electrification, No 70046 (formerly *Anzac* but now devoid of nameplate) heads a late-afternoon departure from Marylebone past Stocking Farm, on its way to Nottingham Victoria.

Again this is an approximation of the view on 16 April 2013, by using bridges and footpaths as markers. *Mike Mitchell, MJS collection/MJS (2)*

ABBEY LANE: Though not unknown, the Class 'L1' 2-6-4Ts were not overly common on this northern part of the GCR, being much more regular motive power at the London end, with many shedded at Neasden. No 67788 looks to be in fine condition externally and internally with a commendable exhaust as it climbs the bank between Abbey Lane Sidings and Belgrave & Birstall with the six-coach 10.05am Rugby Central-Nottingham Victoria stopping train on 31 August 1961. *G. D. King*

Just over three months earlier, No 61421 is seen actually alongside Abbey Lane Sidings, picked out in the delightful late-afternoon light of 17 May 1961, working a Woodford Halse-York fitted freight. Not native to the GCR, it was always a delight to see the occasional 'B16s' on inter-regional freights. A York (50A) loco for the whole of its BR life, it was withdrawn in July 1964 and scrapped at Hughes Bolckow Ltd, Blyth, two months later. *Mike Mitchell, MJS collection*

LEICESTER CENTRAL's northern approaches were on a higher level than the surrounding streets and were a mixture of bridges and brick-retained embankments. Double track to the station throat, the lines then fanned out to encompass a large island platform containing two bays at either end. In July 1966 No 44780 – a Tyseley (Birmingham) incumbent at the time – sweeps past Leicester North Passenger signal box and under the substantial gantry with an afternoon Nottingham Victoria-Marylebone service.

Happily the elevated station site still exists but, like so many other facilities throughout the UK, has been developed. The whole of the complex is now an industrial site of factory units, with the northern end, seen 16 April 2013, being the parking area for one of them. At least the original railway walls are extant. *David Richards/MJS*

LEICESTER CENTRAL: An impressive sight at any location, the appearance of a Stanier 'Pacific' at Leicester Central certainly stirred the blood, as can be judged from the number of enthusiasts running along the platform to obtain a fuller and longer view of the mighty beast. On 9 May 1964 No 46251 *City of Nottingham* slows for the stop 2 minutes early, at 8.02am, at the head of the RCTS 'The East Midlander No 7' rail tour, taking participants from Nottingham Victoria to Didcot behind this loco.

With the exact comparative view blocked at the time of this photograph on 16 April 2013, this is slightly further north along the old platform, with the approximate line of the platform edge being just inside the canopy supporting pillars.
MJS collection/MJS

R.C.T.S.
THE
EAST MIDLANDER

46251

Below: **LEICESTER CENTRAL:** The east and west sides of the station complex, as regards the platform design, were virtually a mirror image of each other. On the western side, No 61455 slowly draws through the station with a down inter-regional fitted freight on 6 May 1960, while an Annesley 9F awaits the semaphore signal to give a clear road north.

Whether for structural reasons is unknown, but there are anomalies at the former Leicester Central, whereby elements of the erstwhile platforms remain, interrupting either the buildings (at the northern end) or the car park (at the south). On 16 April 2013 this sizeable chunk of the down platform certainly makes its presence felt! *Mike Mitchell, MJS collection/MJS*

LEICESTER CENTRAL: Midway along the down (western) Platform 5 at Leicester Central, No 42556 liberally pollutes the surroundings as it waits, with carriage doors still open, to begin its journey as a Leicester Central-Nottingham Victoria local on 25 May 1962. A type of locomotive that would not have been seen under normal conditions on the GCR line before coming under BR(LMR) control in the late 1950s, No 42556, built by the North British Loco Co, became a Leicester Central shed member from 19 March 1960 until withdrawal in August 1963, five months after the cessation of such local trips.

Compared to the last day of through working on the GCR 'London Extension', the last day of the DMU service between Rugby Central and Nottingham Arkwright Street on 3 May 1969 was little covered by photographers. Though not as photogenic as steam, the DMU service is well patronised on this last day, with most of the expectant travellers seeming to be genuine and not there just for this final chance. *Colour-Rail collection/Barry Hilton, MJS collection*

LEICESTER CENTRAL: The bays at the southern end of the station were, again, mirrors of their counterparts at the northern end. On an unidentified date in 1961, but what looks to be around midday in summer, No 44777 stands in the bay with a short rake of box vans awaiting the next duty. The driver casually carries his billycan towards his charge and the station has a generally somnolent air. The sidings to the right and left have a healthy collection of vehicles.

A view of the remains of the down platform and bay at the southern end on 16 April 2013 again present the conundrum of why this was not swept away for the obvious car parking need! Note that two old railway buildings still stand in use on the right, the nearest being the old Central goods office, but the erstwhile Stibbe & Co factory has been demolished and replaced by a more modern construction. *Syd Hancock/MJS*

LEICESTER CENTRAL: To the right of the images on the previous page lay a turntable and water column. On 24 May 1960 ex-works No 61139 takes water from the latter before reversing on to the turntable (just off the picture to the left) to face north ready to take up its next duty. A servant of 41A, Sheffield (Darnall) shed, when seen here, the superb external condition was not to be the precursor to a long service, as it was withdrawn in October 1962.

It is so often amazing ... and disappointing ... how subsequent development can so readily disguise any trace of a railway presence. On 16 April 2013 the car park is nowhere near as aesthetically pleasing as the view of the 'B1'! *Alec Swain, MJS collection/MJS*

BRAUNSTONE GATE: The southern exit from Leicester Central was again above street level and led to bridges over the local roads and the River Soar. This superb lattice girder bowstring bridge took the line over Braunstone Gate and was a much-loved local feature. When photographed on 11 March 1984, 15 years after a train ran over it, it had been converted to a Leicester Corporation footpath. Note the 'Kenning Car & Van Mart' and carpet warehouse to the right.

In 2005 the City Council wished to demolish the bridge, supposedly as it was near the end of its life and struggling to bear its own weight, but local opposition and a brief intimation from the present GCR that it could serve again as a rail access led to a stay of execution. When seen on 24 December 2005 the battle raged and Kenning was still selling cars.

Sadly, so-called progress and development won, and one of the finest examples of this type of bridge was dispatched to oblivion. DeMontfort University might have its Diamond Jubilee Leisure Centre, but the view is now not as attractive, not helped by the demolition of the Kenning building. *All MJS*

LEICESTER NORTH GOODS: With the number of services on the railway and the much greater provision for passengers in pre- and early BR days, storage of carriages was a not uncommon sight. In a delightful view from 6 August 1962, a very smart No 44847 passes the former GCR carriage sheds on the left with a Bank Holiday excursion to Marylebone. Note the use of a Gresley coach immediately behind the loco.

In the view a few yards to the south on 27 September 1970 the sheds have been abandoned and the main running lines in the centre of the view lifted. After Vic Berry had inherited the site for his scrap metal business some years later, he had plans to restore the sheds to more serviceable condition, with a view to storing coaches that he was repainting for BR, but this plan failed to materialise. *G. D. King/M A King, MJS collection*

LEICESTER NORTH GOODS: A few yards further south, with Leicester North Goods signal box still visible in the distance, No 45299 crosses the River Soar with a Nottingham Victoria-Marylebone three-coach semi-fast (8.52am off Leicester) on Saturday 7 August 1965. The carriage sheds are just beyond the rear coach but largely hidden here by the drifting smoke. The huge warehouse on the right still stands prominently. The sidings to the right were the locations for at least two exhibitions by the **LNER.**

The area to the right was acquired and occupied by Vic Berry's scrapyard for many years from the 1980s, retaining one or two lengths of track but largely dispensing with the rest to allow freer access for his machinery. On 30 September 1984 yard shunter No 03069 temporarily rests between duties, whilst **DMU No M53050** alongside awaits the attention of the acetylene torch.
Horace Gamble, MJS collection/MJS

LEICESTER SOUTH GOODS: The boundary between North and South Goods was the large Upperton Road bridge, straddling all four running lines and the sidings. Looking south from the bridge above the former GCR goods yard in November 1985, a BR Class 08 shunter prepares to return to Leicester Midland shed by way of the linking incline to the Burton-upon-Trent line, accessed in the left middle distance, on the far side of the industrial site. After leaving its latest consist in Vic Berry's yard, the journey back is with a single brake-van. The old main line has on the right been converted to the Great Central Way, a public pedestrian/cycleway.

On the ground and looking back towards Leicester Central through the spans of

Upperton Road bridge, two cyclists approach on the Great Central Way. By this time, 24 December 2005, it had been all change again on the far side of the bridge, with Vic Berry's yard closed and new housing built on the abandoned land. The right-hand span had been the main entrance by rail to the scrapyard. *Peter Simmonds/MJS*

LEICESTER SOUTH GOODS: An elevated view, again looking back towards the city, shows **No 60102** *Sir Frederick Banbury* in fine fettle, with plenty of power available to attack the impending 1 in 264 rising gradient from Leicester South Goods on 23 March 1957 with the 11-coach 8.25am Manchester London Road-Marylebone express. To the right, just beyond the signal gantry and signal box, the turnout to Leicester Central loco shed can just be seen. Note the very tall signals, indicating an impending arrival in the opposite direction. *Barry Hilton, MJS collection*

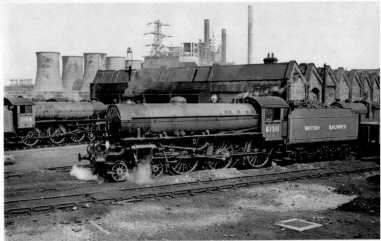

LEICESTER CENTRAL SHED: Arriving at the shed, we have two 'B1s' in a period of transition in 1948. Only months after nationalisation, No 61311 has already received its new BR number, whereas sister loco No 1109 carries its 1946 identity. At this stage they are both still in their LNER 'Apple Green' liveries. The shed, with its northlight roofing and clock above the foreman's office, is typical of many on the GCR. Leicester's power station looms in the background. *MJS collection*

LEICESTER CENTRAL SHED, unlike many, remained basically unaltered throughout its life. Opened in 1897, in connection with the construction of the GCR line south to London, the four-road shed boasted a coaling stage, water tank and turntable. Allocated the code 38C by BR in 1948, it became 15E on 1 February 1958 after absorption by BR(LMR) and was closed on 6 July 1964. Home to many famous and iconic engines over the years, No 46140 *The King's Royal Rifle Corps* is the celebrity in this undated portrait. In view of its majestic condition and the fact that it wears a 14B (Kentish Town) shedplate, it could well be May 1961, when Leicester City played Tottenham Hotspur in the FA Cup Final, and it may be waiting to take its turn on the fast run to London over the GCR.

Another feature of many GCR sheds was the presence of sheerlegs, utilised to lift locomotives from the track for inspection. Whether the celebrated gas turbine loco No GT3 was here for attention on 21 May 1961 is unknown, but the uniqueness of the loco in this position, in bright sunshine, was a godsend for the photographer. *Colour-rail collection/Les Wade, MJS collection*

LEICESTER SOUTH GOODS: Early morning and late afternoon light is the magic time for photographers, especially those seeking heightened definition in black and white. A superb example is this view of 'B16/3' No 1406 as it restarts its long mixed unfitted freight from Leicester South Goods. Renumbered from its 1946 persona to 61406 on 21 September 1948, it was again renumbered, to 61475, in 1950, with the extension of the construction of 'B1s' up to 61409. Probably in the late 1940s, the loco has obviously been working hard for some time as evidenced by the scorched smokebox front. *MJS collection*

Across the tracks and looking south, No 61271 passes Leicester South Goods signal box in June 1960 with the 5.05pm Woodford Halse-Leicester Central working, sporting the 'Ordinary Passenger' headcode. The Central shed building and yard can be seen in the left distance. *Mike Mitchell, MJS collection*

LEICESTER SOUTH GOODS: LNER 'K3s' were not rare on the GCR but were not overly common, more usually found on inter-regional freights. One such is No 61843, heading a mixed freight past the Leicester South Goods signal box around 1956/57. Another successful design from Nigel Gresley, as a development of a Great Northern type, the first was introduced in 1924 and the class served both LNER and BR well until their eventual demise in the early 1960s. Allocated to Woodford Halse from September 1956, '43' was dispensed with in November 1962.

One of the reasons for the disappearance of the 'K3s' from both ex-GCR and LNER lines was the influx of BR Standard 9Fs from the late 1950s. Ten of the early ones were built in 1955 to an altered design by two Italian State Railway engineers, modifying the conventional fire-tube boiler by what was effectively a secondary boiler. These locos were fitted with side-mounted chimneys and, initially, a second smokebox door. Not being hugely successful, the 'Crostis', as they were more commonly known, were eventually converted to a more standard arrangement but without the smoke deflectors employed by the rest of the class. In 'standard' mode, No 92021 leads its mixed fitted freight past the signal box in the spring of 1964. *Milepost 92½, railphotolibrary.com/MJS collection*

LEICESTER SOUTH GOODS: A view from the footpath along the backs of the houses on the west side of the line sees No 44846 beginning to pick up speed as it approaches the rising 1 in 246 gradient past the tracks on the right leading to the engine shed. The image is undated, but the loco was an Annesley servant from 9 March 1963 to 31 July 1965. The wood yard on the right looks to be in great demand, judging by the piles of timber stacked up alongside the railway.

Less than a decade later the wood yard is still in good business, but not so the railway. A year after the end of the Rugby-Nottingham DMU service, the abandonment and desecration of the railway is plain to see, with the remains of the main line being grassed over. The line to the right, however, was still in use, bringing stock to the yard beyond Upperton Road bridge in the distance that was eventually fully employed by either or both Vic and Frank Berry. *MJS collection/Mike Mitchell, MJS collection*

LEICESTER SOUTH GOODS: A
further eight years have passed and
though the vantage point is the same
as in the previous pictures, and the
vista recognisable, there are still
changes. On 29 November 1978 the
main-line track has been lifted and
nature is obliterating traces, but the
track to the scrapyard is still in situ
and the woodyard is still working
hard.

And so to July 1996. The Great
Central Way has been constructed
by Leicester Council and follows the
trajectory of the erstwhile main line,
but elsewhere there are no traces left
of the old permanent way. Just visible
over the trees, however, are signs
that the woodyard battles on, but
by this date the Berry scrapyard has
been cleared, following the disastrous
fire a few years earlier. *Both Peter
Simmonds*

MARLOW ROAD: Now heading
for the outer reaches of the city,
the line is again graced by railway
royalty. With excitement among the
linesiders, preserved No 4472 (aka
No 60103) *Flying Scotsman* accelerates
south at 12.15pm on 18 April 1964,
after a water stop at Leicester
South Goods, with the Stephenson
Locomotive Society (North West
Area)/Manchester Locomotive Society
'Great Central Railway Rail Tour'.
Beginning from Manchester Central
station at 8.28am, the 'A3' ran the
whole tour to Marylebone and then
back up the GCR to Penistone, from
where electric loco No E26052 took
over back to Manchester.

The same aspect on 16 April 2013
would not give you any hint of there
having been a railway here. The Great
Central Way continues, but not on
the course of the old main line, and
the surrounding area has been totally
re-landscaped. The houses seen in
the earlier view are hidden from view
by the growth of trees over the last
decade. *MJS collection/MJS*

AYLESTONE: Progressing south, the GCR passes over river and canal several times as it courses through Leicester, and here, on the leafy southern outskirts, it crosses the Leicestershire & Northamptonshire Union Canal at Aylestone on a distinctly sturdy bridge. On Wednesday 13 July 1966 No 44835 climbs the 1 in 408 with a Nottingham Victoria-Rugby Central local (8.20am off Leicester). *Horace Gamble, MJS collection*

Double-heading was not common on the GCR, but the sight of two ex-GWR 'Halls' on the line was unusual in the extreme! Presumably using the working as a means of returning one of the locomotives to the Western Region, Nos 6979 *Helperly Hall* and 4933 *Himley Hall* are still climbing on their way out of the city and working hard, although their consist would surely not trouble one locomotive, let alone two! *John Clay, MJS collection*

WHETSTONE, between Wigston and Narborough, saw the meeting of the **GCR** line and the ex-**LMS** Nuneaton-Leicester line, the former crossing over the latter. Seen from the local Blaby-Enderby road overbridge, No 44941 heads south away from Leicester on an unidentified date in June 1966, with the 6.15pm Nottingham Victoria-Rugby semi-fast.

The roles are now reversed, as we see No 170106 heading south-west away from Leicester with CrossCountry's 1N55, the 1227 Stansted Airport to Birmingham New Street semi-fast, on 16 April 2013. The view is slightly to the left of the earlier one, as more recent road and bridge alterations have changed the vantage point, but it is gratifying to see that the GCR bridge is still in situ, accommodating walkers and cyclists along the old trackbed. *Mike Mitchell, MJS collection/MJS*

WHETSTONE, like other stations we have already seen, had an island platform, with the same basic GCR provision and architecture. The embankment seen on the previous page continued across fields into the station, and this view is taken from a footpath at a slightly lower level than the rails. Again on an unnamed date in June 1966, No 44941 heads north with the 4.38pm Marylebone-Nottingham Victoria train, but will not be stopping, as the station closed in 1963 together with other local stations on the line.

With the embankment at what was the station site now breached by new housing and the adjacent footpath fence blocked from view by years of verdant growth, this is a view from the foot of the embankment on 16 April 2013, looking towards the old site. *Mike Mitchell, MJS collection/MJS*

ASHBY MAGNA: A brave attempt to introduce a possible gas turbine express locomotive to the UK's railways saw **No GT3** run trials over the GCR, and one such test, from Rugby Central to Leicester Central, was captured on film entering Ashby Magna at 4.11pm on 21 September 1961.

The majority of the station site, between the platforms and a tunnel some half a mile to the south, is now given over to a woodyard, but with the northern third left barren. A comparative view on 16 April 2013 has that yard beyond the trees. All that is left of the GCR are some random bricks embedded within the currently abandoned land seen here. *Mike Mensing/MJS, with permission of the landowner*

ASHBY MAGNA: Further along the lineside, a few yards to the south, the layout of Ashby Magna station, looking north, is more clearly seen on 25 July 1959 as No 61804 passes through with a Newcastle-Bournemouth cross-country inter-regional express. The island layout is well illustrated, as are the sidings and very open countryside in which the station was situated. Although the loco was shedded at Woodford Halse at this date and was no doubt returning to its home, the sight of a 'K3' on these workings was not common, with York 'V2s' the more usual fare.

Again the site now looks like a wasteland, with the 'landscaping' showing the rise up to the road in the earlier view but the trees now hiding it from sight on 16 April 2013. *Barry Hilton/MJS, with permission of the landowner*

ASHBY MAGNA is seen again on the very last day, 3 September 1966. No 45292, now stripped of its front numberplate, speeds south through the station and past the signal box with the 1115 Nottingham Victoria-Marylebone train. The signalman watches from his box, but the scene is notable for there not being any other visible witnesses of this memorable event. The loco is adorned with an unofficial 'THE LAST DAY GREAT CENTRAL' message on the smokebox.

The aforementioned woodyard is now seen in something of its full glory on 16 April 2013, taking full advantage of the wide land area inherited from the railway. The former signal box stood alongside the site of the tall mast, and its recess still exists, whilst the yard surface is made up of what look to be old concrete sleepers. *Bryan Hicks/MJS, with permission of the landowner*

DUNTON BASSETT TUNNEL, otherwise known as Ashby Tunnel, just 92 yards long, was immediately south of Ashby Magna station, and this view shows the southern portal. On 29 August 1959 No 60842 emerges with a through inter-regional train to the South Coast, including in the consist two ancient-looking ex-Southern coaches. A resident of 38C (Leicester Central shed) at the time, the 'V2' had no doubt relieved a northern loco at Leicester and would work through to at least Oxford. Moving to York shed two weeks after this view, it was withdrawn in November 1962.

At the same location but across the tracks, celebrity No 4472

Flying Scotsman emerges from the tunnel on 15 June 1963 with the RPS Sheffield-Marylebone 'Great Central Special' complete with headboard. The loco handled the tour in both directions, with then owner Alan Pegler on board. *Both Barry Hilton*

LUTTERWORTH: After their introduction the English Electric Type 3s saw usage on the GCR on the North East to South inter-regional rosters, giving spotters a distinct variety compared with the predominantly BR(LMR) fare present in the early 1960s. One such example is No D6749, seen on Saturday 22 May 1965 with the 10.50am Bournemouth West-York train just north of Lutterworth station, which can be glimpsed in the distance. Viewed from the road to Gilmorton, an empty M1 is on the left, with the signpost and bridge for the junction for Lutterworth. The removal of the siding has resulted in a long loop on the western edge of the line.

With the earlier view since obliterated by housing, we move to the south of town, station and motorway junction on 16 April 2013. The shallow cutting, in a dip between two gradients, is still identifiable as former railway land in this view from the road to Swinford, despite more motorcycle scrambling, and the proximity of the M1 is still retained, just visible upper left. *Mike Mensing/MJS*

RUGBY CENTRAL: The West Coast Main Line, its station at Rugby and the GCR overbridge are all on the northern edge of the town. Some quarter of a mile to the south the latter railway approached the Central station in a cutting. Leaving Rugby Central on Saturday 24 April 1965, No 45215 accelerates at the beginning of a falling 1 in 176 gradient with the 2.38pm Marylebone-Nottingham Victoria six-coach semi-fast, the footplate crewman again posing for his portrait.

The progress of passing years has attempted to regain the former trackbed, but thankfully a semblance of previous pathways is retained by an official cycleway and footpath. The old station site is partially screened by tree growth in this view on 16 April 2013; access to the path from the road is identified by the railing. *Mike Mensing/MJS*

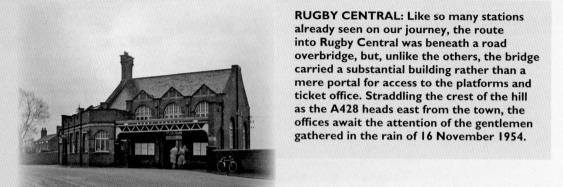

RUGBY CENTRAL: Like so many stations already seen on our journey, the route into Rugby Central was beneath a road overbridge, but, unlike the others, the bridge carried a substantial building rather than a mere portal for access to the platforms and ticket office. Straddling the crest of the hill as the A428 heads east from the town, the offices await the attention of the gentlemen gathered in the rain of 16 November 1954.

One year after closure, the buildings still stand but with the doors resolutely closed as a weak winter sun on 8 March 1970 shines on the brickwork, the snow and the roadway, now adorned with a broken white line. The phone box remains for needy callers.

Forward 43 years, and the A428 is decidedly busier, now with a central bollard to assist crossing pedestrians when seen on 16 April 2013. The buildings have gone but their former presence can be identified by the newer and differently coloured brickwork in the retaining wall and the newly angled wall at this end. *Keith Jones collection/Bryan Hicks/MJS*

RUGBY CENTRAL: Down on the platform, No 45324 arrives at precisely 9.30am on 5 March 1966 with the 0815 Nottingham Victoria-Marylebone semi-fast. One solitary worker and a staff member witness the arrival at the northern end of the platform, and it is quite possible that the number elsewhere would not have been great. A much travelled loco, the 'Black 5' spent most of its working life on the WCML before transfer to Annesley on 19 February 1966, just two weeks before this view.

The absence of the station buildings is obvious in this view from 16 April 2013. The former entrance and stairway have been bricked over and have received unwanted graffiti. The erstwhile trackbeds, on both sides of the central platform, have been partially infilled and, with both north and south ends being stopped with an earth bank, the platforms are now bordered by semi-stagnant ponds! *Bryan Hicks/MJS*

RUGBY CENTRAL: On the bright sunny morning of 11 September 1960, a distinctly healthy congregation waits at the station. It would have been good if normal services were this popular, but the gathering bodies await the arrival of the RCTS (East Midlands Branch) 'East Midlander No 4 Rail Tour'. The participants eagerly await the train, due at 9.27am, which will be hauled as far as Oxford, on its way to Eastleigh and Swindon, by preserved Midland Railway 'Compound' No 1000. Note the raised siding on the left with a rake of tarpaulined timber. The manner in which the station buildings sat atop the platforms can more clearly be seen in this view.

Remarkably this is the same vista on 16 April 2013, now dramatically disguised by the landscaping for the cycleway/footpath, the only tangible clue being the rising slope in the path as it climbs to the former platform. The end of the ponds on both sides is at this point. *K. Fairey/ Colour-Rail collection/MJS*

RUGBY CENTRAL: On a bright summer afternoon in July 1955, a smart **No 60102** *Sir Frederick Banbury* looks the part with 'head held high' at full speed down the 1 in 330 gradient as it approaches Rugby Central with a northbound express. A huge water tower can just be glimpsed above the first coach, and the whole is witnessed by the sturdy brick-built signal box. The lengthman has certainly done his job well judging by the clean and tidy permanent way. *MJS collection*

Most definitely a rare sight at Rugby Central on Sunday 7 September 1958 is **No D201**, the second of the class and then just four months old. It is restarting from the station at the head of the 9.51am Royal Observe Corps 'Farnborough Flyer' rail tour from Retford to Farnborough and back. Becoming **No 40001** under the **TOPS** renumbering of 1973, it succumbed to the cutter's torch in 1984. *Mike Mensing*

RUDDINGTON: On a gloriously sunny 11 May 2002, No 61248 *Geoffrey Gibbs* **(actually No 61264 in disguise) stands as a prime exhibit at the Nottingham Transport Heritage Centre, Ruddington. New in March 1948, to East Anglia, No 61264 became a** GCR resident in December 1960 with a move to 40E (Colwick) shed. The changes wrought by dieselisation and the predominance of ex-LMS locomotives on the GCR led to its early demise, on 11 December 1965, at just 17 years old. *Michael Mason, MJS collection*

Among a sizeable collection of diesel locos at Nottingham Transport Heritage Centre, on 13 April 2013 No 47292 stands in company with Nos 46010 and 56097, displaying differing front-end designs. *MJS*

LOUGHBOROUGH CENTRAL: As this was being written, the long-held dream of reunifying the two halves of the private GCR, by 'bridging the gap' over the Midland Main Line at Loughborough Midland station, was making great strides towards becoming a reality. This was the view at the northern extremity of the southern section on 14 August 1994, with the course of the lost trackbed indicated by the pathway enjoyed by the walkers.

Looking in the opposite direction on 31 October 2007, the view is towards the current engine shed, showing some clearance on the bridge deck and buildings and stock on the line of the old route. *Both MJS*

Again seen on 31 October 2007, the railway's railbus is in a parlous state, graphically showing some of the challenges that face the preservationists! With restoration to working order obviously not imminent, a fresh home will have to be found when the rails return to this site over the next few years. *MJS*

LOUGHBOROUGH CENTRAL SHED: As preserved railways develop, they rapidly realise the need for covered accommodation for both running stock and those items needing restoration. By the time of this scene in 1974, the 'new' GCR had constructed a cat's cradle of steelwork that would eventually become the engine shed at Loughborough. On the right the photographer's wife surveys the task ahead, not least the work required on the hulk of No 71000 *Duke of Gloucester*, which many a doom-monger had predicted was a lost cause. The stalwarts of the restoration team proved them all wrong!

By 27 January 2013 the scene is very different. The corrugated iron shed has now served for approaching 40 years, and stock, sundry buildings and other detritus litter the yard. Again, the closure of the gap to the northern section will sweep all this away. *Both MJS*

LOUGHBOROUGH CENTRAL SHED: Three boilers await further attention outside the shed on 11 August 2004. The first, on jacks, belongs to the 1925 Urie-designed 'King Arthur' Class No 30777 *Sir Lamiel*. One of the National Railway Museum collection, the loco has seen many years 'out in the field'.

Adjacent, the boiler of Stanier 'Black 5' No 45231 is also jacked up, but this time in steam. New in 1936 from Armstrong Whitworth, it has worn the name *The Sherwood Forester* in preservation. It was a long-time resident on the GCR before being sold to new owners. Main-line registered, it can now often be found on the West Highland line in Scotland and, when not in use, it tends to reside at Carnforth.

The elder statesman of the trio, Gresley Class 'N2' No 69523, is behind *Sir Lamiel*, on yet more jacks. Built in 1921, it was one of 107 built, initially for the GNR, which numbered it 1744. It became No 4744 under the LNER 1923 renumbering, then 9523 in 1946. *All MJS*

LOUGHBOROUGH CENTRAL SHED: Outside the shed, facing towards Loughborough Central station, 'West Country' 4-6-2 No 34039 *Boscastle* is now in full glory and is the centre of attention, in company with 'Black 5' No 5231 on 14 August 1994. *MJS*

On the last day of its visit to the Great Central Railway, Sunday 22 March 2009, 'Q6' 0-8-0 No 63395 rests on shed just before its next turn out on the line, being subjected to a quick visual check by the crew on another bright sunny day. *MJS*

LOUGHBOROUGH CENTRAL SHED: Like many other private railways over the past four decades, early tracks and motive power were both short in length and a motley collection of 'anything that can run'. Moving beyond the road bridge, it can be seen that *King Haakon VII* is decidedly *not* British in design and presents a complete novelty as operated by the GCR in 1974. Known as Prince Carl of Denmark until 1905, Haakon was the first king of Norway after the 1905 dissolution of the personal union with Sweden. Regarded in Norway as one of the greatest Norwegians of the 20th century, he is particularly revered for his courage during the German invasion and for his leadership and preservation of Norwegian unity during the Nazi occupation. He died at the age of 85 on 21 September 1957, having reigned for nearly 52 years. The loco has more lately been on the Nene Valley Railway.

By contrast, 21 years later on 3 February 1995, we have a personification of an iconic British loco, a 'Jubilee' 4-6-0 in the guise of No 5552 *Silver Jubilee*, in LMS black livery complete with raised letters and numerals. The true identity of the locomotive was No 45593 *Kolhapur*. *Both MJS*

LOUGHBOROUGH CENTRAL SHED: At the same location the date has come forward but the vintage of the loco has gone back! 1888-vintage Webb 'Coal Tank' No 1054 spent much of 2012/13 travelling the country visiting various preserved railways and in various guises. On 18 April 2013 it has reached Loughborough Central, delivered that afternoon ready for a series of passenger and freight runs over the GCR, looking diminutive against both the coach and the 08 shunter. *MJS*

Viewed from the public footpath to the west of the tracks, one of the crew of No 37198, in Network Rail yellow livery, chats with a visitor while awaiting the next duty on Sunday 13 May 2012. The loco came to the GCR from Network Rail, which still owns it, for contract body repairs and painting into the standard yellow NR colour scheme some years ago. 'Peak' No D123 stands behind in BR green. *MJS*

LOUGHBOROUGH CENTRAL SHED: Turning the clock way back in preservation terms, in the bare and open yard between the shed and the station at Loughborough Central newly arrived No 34039 *Boscastle* announces the laudable ambition of 'The Return of Steam' in April 1973. Note the white boots, so fashionable at the time. Withdrawn from 71A (Eastleigh shed) in May 1965, the loco found itself inside Barry scrapyard by the end of the year. It was there for nearly eight years, before being bought privately by Mr J. Tawse and moved in January 1973 to the GCR.

A further two decades saw restoration to the remarkable transformation seen outside the shed on 31 August 1993. In fine external condition, the polish on the boiler picks up the yellow reflections from the railway's infrastructure machines. *MJS/John Morgan, MJS collection*

LOUGHBOROUGH CENTRAL SHED: During 2013 Leicester enjoyed celebrity status following the discovery of the buried remains of King Richard III. By good fortune, preserved 'King' 4-6-0 No 6023 was visiting the GCR and the local King Richard III Society booked the loco to haul a special dining train. As mentioned on page 52, the GCR locos normally face south but, renumbered and renamed No 6015 *King Richard III*, the 4-6-0 was turned for Michael Portillo. Seen in the late afternoon sunshine of Friday 19 April 2013, preparations are complete and the loco waits for the road to Central station and its dining train.

Fifty years after the original No 6015 was withdrawn, from 84A (Wolverhampton Stafford Road shed), a *King Richard III* nameplate once more graces the driving wheel splasher of an ex-GWR 'King'. *Both MJS*

LOUGHBOROUGH CENTRAL: The two decades since the state of affairs glimpsed on page 103 saw massive strides in progress and development at Loughborough Central station, with both the utilisation of remaining BR structures and the creation and provision of design features to enhance the visitor experience and maintain the heightened requirements for safety of those visitors, together with staff and volunteers. On 31 August 1993 ex-GWR No 5224, totally artificially wearing a 38A (Colwick) shedplate, drifts into the platform before taking its place at the head of the next departure. *John Morgan, MJS collection*

At the opposite end of the platform No 78019 waits for the road as the 1000 departure for Leicester North on 22 March 2009. Another Barry resident from 1967 until March 1973, after withdrawal from Crewe South shed in November 1966, its first port of call following rescue was the Severn Valley Railway, but it was later restored to steam at Loughborough. *MJS*

LOUGHBOROUGH CENTRAL: Great Central Road, outside the station entrance, provides fine views of the line as it heads south. Once again the view changed over the years as money and ideas dictated refinements, and this view from relatively early days sees *Littleton No 5* approaching with the last train of day from Quorn in October 1977, with just the running tracks in place.

The ensuing 24 years saw redesign of the trackwork, providing sidings on either side of the main running lines and enabling the railway to store some of its stock for easy access. On 2 July 2011 newly renumbered 50-year-old Class 10 shunter No 10119 (previously D4067), in a magnificent blue coat with a red-backed *Margaret Ethel – Thomas Alfred Naylor* nameplate, stands ready for its next duty. *Peter Simmonds/MJS*

LOUGHBOROUGH CENTRAL: Thankfully, two locomotives have survived from the original GCR. New from Gorton Works in 1919 as one of the Robinson 'Improved Director' Class '11F' 4-4-0s, the preserved No 506 *Butler-Henderson* was formerly a resident of the **NRM** in York, but more latterly has spent time at **Barrow Hill Roundhouse** together with visits to private railways, including the present GCR. This glorious b&w view from 18 November 1989, with a Gresley coach to the right, is almost timeless, with the loco wearing its original GCR number and a facsimile of the company logo on the tender, as it storms out of Loughborough Central with a southbound 'express'. The first coach behind the locomotive is another GCR survivor, one of the few remaining 'Barnum' coaches; it is now awaiting restoration at Ruddington.

The view from Beeches Road, south of the station, also provides a fine vantage point, not least to the north, with the prevailing light behind the photographer, and there are opportunities for some spirited exits from the station, seen in the background. On 30 July 2004 an immaculately turned-out No 45305 looks the part as it recreates a Marylebone express, gathering speed with the seven-coach 1030 departure to Leicester North. *Tom Heavyside/MJS*

LOUGHBOROUGH CENTRAL: Two more views from Beeches Road bridge show the development of the track layout on the exit from the station. In the first, from 15 August 1997, No 92212 makes a leisurely departure from the down platform with a recreated 'Windcutter' rake of wagons. Sidings have been laid on both sides of the running lines and a new 'main line' is being laid, to give greater flexibility and enable enhanced services.

Eleven years later, another BR Standard is in charge, but this time with passenger stock and making a far more explosive image. Looking as though it is wearing 'mutton chop' whiskers, No 70013 *Oliver Cromwell* accelerates, with steam cocks blowing, as the 1200 departure to Leicester North,

'The South Yorkshireman', on 5 May 2008. A lineside photographer, hidden from view by the steam, would not have captured a particularly worthwhile shot! Note that the second running line is now in use, together with a crossover between the two lines. *Both MJS*

LOUGHBOROUGH CENTRAL: Here are two more views from Beeches Road, but this time looking south. A fine gantry of semaphores is much more attractive than colour lights; they present style and add ambience to a scene, as well as still giving an indication of approaching traffic from the reverse side! On the southern approach to Loughborough Central station, No 78019 nears the end of its journey as the 1425 train from Leicester North on Sunday 26 August 2012.

Eighteen months earlier No 5526 rattles along towards Loughborough with an auto-coach, the 0947 service from Rothley, during the GCR's 'Winter Steam Gala' on Saturday 29 January 2011. Visiting from the South Devon Railway, the 1928-vintage 2-6-2T is obviously keen to give the photographers some value with its backlit exhaust. *Both MJS*

WOODTHORPE: On a bright and sunny 14 August 1994, No 4498 *Sir Nigel Gresley*, in glorious Garter Blue livery, hurries away from Loughborough under the A6 road bridge and towards Woodthorpe with the 1400 train to Leicester North. It is accelerating from a slack for the temporary A6 bridge work, the scaffolding for which can be seen in the background, taking advantage of the railway being single track at this stage.

While steam is predominantly the main attraction for the visiting public, diesel locomotives and multiple units have their own interest; more prosaically, they have their real uses to the operating railway, not least in running services when patronage may not be anticipated to be great. A two-car DMU forms the 1430 Loughborough Central-Rothley service on 5 May 2008, with both tracks now in use. *Both MJS*

QUORN & WOODHOUSE: Retrospective visions can often be enlightening, stirring the ashes of a faded memory. In this view from 1974 at Quorn, *Littleton No 5* draws to a halt, seeming somewhat incongruous at the head of ex-BR blue and grey coaches. Note how bare the platform appears and, while the surroundings are open, nature is trying hard not to lose its grip. There is yet but little in the yard.

The remarkable feat of recreating an LNER 'A1' 'Pacific' from scratch has amazed many millions in the UK and elsewhere and awoken a latent interest in railways in general and steam in particular among the populous. As part of its 'running in', touring the country to 'spread the word', No 60163 *Tornado* pauses with the 1200 Loughborough Central-Leicester North working on 22 September 2008. Three decades of progress on the ground and tree growth on the far boundary have dramatically altered the feel of this once quiet halt. *Both MJS*

QUORN & WOODHOUSE: Lost property is an ongoing problem for Network Rail and the Rail Operating Companies, but for private railways past detritus can make for wonderful exhibits. Tucked away under the footbridge at Quorn on 2 July 2011, this gem even includes a spare stockinged leg! *MJS*

With its double track and 'main-line' status, the GCR has been able to offer space and time for outside organisations to trial and test various stock and systems. On 10 March 2006 resident No 37255, in fading 'Dutch' livery, is on brake-testing duties for Network Rail, utilising the tracks at Quorn. Alongside is the railway's own 'Rat', No 25265, the whole giving the appearance of a busy goods yard on the main UK network. *MJS*

QUORN & WOODHOUSE:
Another example of the
testing facilities available
from the GCR is the presence
of a road-rail Unimog
demonstrating its capabilities
at Quorn for ballast disposal
on 16 June 1999. This was not
specifically for the benefit of
the GCR, but for potential
clients of Amey Fleet Services,
although it had the knock-
on bonus of improving the
condition of the private
company's main line. *MJS*

A demonstration of a different nature was the operation of a
Travelling Post Office on 30 October 1982. During a special
diesel weekend (!), No 506 *Butler-Henderson* attacks what
was then the single line immediately south of Quorn station,
moments before the hanging bag is caught by the mail train
pick-up at speed. Again notice the open feel of the site at this
stage of the railway's development. *MJS*

SWITHLAND RESERVOIR: One of the features on the run from Loughborough to Belgrave & Birstall is the crossing of bridges over the usually tranquil waters at Swithland Reservoir. As travel options have progressed over the years, dining trains on the current **GCR** often stand on the bridges while the meals are served to the accompaniment of peace and duck calls! In earlier times, No 5231 *The Sherwood Forester*, in pseudo **LMS** livery, sweeps around the curve and onto the first bridge with a southbound train on 10 October 1976.

At the same location in September 1983 but travelling in the opposite direction, with a northbound service, is No D9523. New from Swindon Works in December 1964, its initial allocation was 81A (Old Oak Common shed), but it lasted on BR for just 3½ years, being withdrawn from Hull in April 1968! Initially preserved on the GCR, the 21st century saw it on the NVR in maroon livery. The down line has been lifted, with only the up remaining in both photographs. *Tom Heavyside/Peter Johnson*

SWITHLAND SIDINGS: Another major development over the past three decades has been the progressive enlargement and enhancement of the sidings at Swithland, complete with the installation of new signal box to control the main lines and sidings. On 23 June 2012 the other survivor from original GCR days, No 63601, eschews its more natural freight role to attend to hauling a Leicester North-Loughborough Central passenger turn as it passes the majestic semaphore signals at Swithland Sidings. Originally built as GCR No 102, one of Robinson's Class '8K' 2-8-0s, in 1911, it lasted on BR until July 1963.

On the same day, but travelling in the opposite direction, ex-BR 'Peak' No D123 *Leicestershire and Derbyshire Yeomanry* is nicely framed by the semaphore sentinels. New from Crewe Works in October 1961, to Derby shed, it became No 45125 in April 1975 and saw rejection at Tinsley depot in May 1987. *Both Syd Hancock*

ROTHLEY: A cause for celebration – on its first trip out following restoration, 'Jinty' No 47406 steams away from Swithland Sidings and approaches its destination as the 0935 Loughborough-Rothley 'local' on Saturday 30 January 2010, during the GCR's 'Lostock & Several Smoking Barrels' three-day gala. New in 1926, it was 40 years old when withdrawn from Edge Hill (Liverpool) shed in December 1966, and it here looks in magnificent condition following its return to steam.

Never put your camera away! In pouring rain, lineside spectators are conspicuous by their absence as No 33002 *Sea King* is captured at the same location, but viewed from Station Road, as it approaches Rothley with the 1400 Loughborough Central-Leicester North service on Sunday 3 June 2012. More normally based on the South Devon Railway, this was the loco's first visit to the GCR. *Both MJS*

ROTHLEY: As already described elsewhere, No 6023 *King Edward II* was turned to face north for a visit to the **GCR** by Michael Portillo on Saturday 13 April 2013. Later in the day this provided a rare view of the 'King' heading boiler-first towards Loughborough as it leaves Rothley station in pouring rain on its last service of the day, the 1655 from Leicester North. It was failed on arrival at Loughborough shed! Again there were no hoards of lineside witnesses at this spot. *MJS*

As well as providing testing facilities for infrastructure companies, locomotive testing has also provided revenue. Trips from Brush Engineering in Loughborough have been and are ongoing, even including some of the foreign diesels built at that factory. On 11 October 1995 DRS No 20302, newly converted from ex-BR No 20084, is coupled to the railway's own Class 20, No D8098, for a test run to Loughborough, prior to its release to traffic. *MJS*

ROTHLEY: Continuing the blue theme, No 4498 *Sir Nigel Gresley* stands proudly in Rothley station on 13 August 1994, not looking at all out of place despite the fact that the type was an extremely rare visitor to the erstwhile GCR. New from Doncaster Works in 1937, as LNER No 4498, it became No 7 in the 1946 renumbering scheme, then 60007 after the 1948 nationalisation. After just short of 30 years hauling crack expresses between King's Cross and Scotland, withdrawal came in February 1966 at 61B (Aberdeen Ferryhill shed). *MJS*

Preservation has brought a wide selection of locomotives to the GCR that would not have been seen on the route under normal circumstances. While ex-GWR 'Halls' were not unknown on trains such as the South to North East cross-country services, No 4953 *Pitchford Hall*, in its near spotless external condition, would not have been a regular sight. On 2 July 2011 it pauses at Rothley with the 1315 Loughborough Central-Leicester North roster, including a Restaurant Car to serve meals during a stop on Swithland Reservoir. *MJS*

ROTHLEY: Six months after the view of *Pitchford Hall* on the previous page, the loco is still providing front-line haulage on 28 January 2012 as it leaves with yet another Loughborough Central-Leicester North service, masquerading as 'The Cornishman' express, a great many miles away from that train's normal route! Note the incredible number of witnesses on the platform and heads poking out of virtually every window! *Syd Hancock*

Many preserved locos have worn coats of many colours over their years in private hands, but certainly unusual was the pseudo LMS 'Crimson Lake' livery allocated to ex-LMS No 8624 when it was returned to steam by Peak Rail in 2009. The only surviving Southern-built 8F, this livery was never worn by freight locomotives and caused some strong comments at the time. Resident on the GCR since 2011, most now seem to have accepted the situation. On 28 January 2012 it storms into Rothley from the south on a demonstration mixed freight train. *Syd Hancock*

THURCASTON: Much of the route between Rothley and Birstall is, as far as photographs go, something of a no-man's-land, with limited opportunities for worthwhile shots. On 7 September 2006, seen from the abutments of the A46 road bridge at Thurcaston, the photographer copes well to capture No 35030 *Elder Dempster Lines*, returning to the GCR and recreating the last-day special as seen on page 29, complete with appropriate headboard. The rear of the train has just passed over the bridge spanning Rothley Brook. The consist of Southern green coaches would have also been familiar to the loco from past days on the SR.

Slightly closer to Rothley, another 'Merchant Navy', No 35005 *Canadian Pacific*, heads south on an unidentified date during a visit to the line. Initially an example of Bulleid's air-smoothed design in 1941 as No 21C5, it was rebuilt to this more standard shape in May 1959. Withdrawn from Weymouth in October 1965, it was quickly transhipped to Barry scrapyard the following January. Rescue came from a private purchaser in March 1973, with a move to Steamtown, Carnforth. The signal in the picture is Rothley's up Section signal. *Syd Hancock/Peter Thwaites, MJS collection*

BELGRAVE & BIRSTALL: The view north from Greengate Lane in Birstall is not over-favoured by photographers, largely due to the near-tunnel effect of the surrounding tree growth that severely restricts the view and times when the light will be accommodating. The strict north-south alignment also militates against a southbound view, looking towards the sunlight. However, the challenge does create some rewards. On its first weekend on the GCR, visiting from the North Norfolk Railway, No 65462 displays effort as it approaches Birstall on 18 January 2004 with its train from Loughborough Central.

No pyrotechnics, but No D5830 still attracts in its BR experimental ochre livery on 29 July 2007 as it brings the 1500 Loughborough Central-Leicester North service towards its destination. *Both MJS*

GREAT CENTRAL RAILWAY
LOUGHBOROUGH, LEICESTERSHIRE

LEICESTER NORTH: As mentioned earlier, Belgrave & Birstall station had an island platform, in company with other similar facilities on the GCR. While those at Quorn & Woodhouse and Rothley have been superbly restored and returned to public use, the station at Birstall was the subject of progressive vandalism during the early 1970s, to the extent that there was effectively no way that a like-for-like restoration could have been achieved. A solitary side platform is all that is currently available to receive trains at the new Leicester North, as seen from Station Road on 5 May 2005. No 70013 *Oliver Cromwell* rests, having arrived with the 1200 service from Loughborough Central.

RE-CREATING THE EXPERIENCE

The same location but a totally different image! No 30777 *Sir Lamiel* has run round its train and prepares to begin the return journey to Loughborough on 26 January 2013, with a sudden flurry of snow still lying on the ground. Hopes and plans have been put forward for an extension from here into Leicester, beyond the buffer stops, as far as Abbey Lane, but the gap is likely to prove too wide. However, a proposed museum in the area to the left of the station will go some way to overcome that loss. *Both MJS*

LEICESTER NORTH is seen again in its very early days, without waiting shelter or other passenger facilities. **No 6990** *Witherslack Hall* halts on 17 July 1991 with its first train of the day from Loughborough Central during the summer's Tuesday-Thursday extra trains. The bricked-up former entrance to Belgrave & Birstall station on Station Road is clearly visible, as is the newly laid track.

Twelve days earlier, on 5 July, a large crowd has gathered to celebrate the opening of the Leicester North platform, with dignitaries past and present holding court. No **35005** *Canadian Pacific* and its train provide the backdrop.

Celebrity was also present at the event and, to the delight of the assembled throng, **Michael Heseltine** mounts the steps to the podium, cheerfully clutching a large cheque (in size and amount) for **£110,000**, a very welcome 'present' from **HM Paymaster General!** *MJS/Peter Thwaites, MJS collection (2)*

LEICESTER NORTH: A decade after the opening of the platform, the terminus has a new station building. Seen on 23 December 2001, the basic structure is in place and ready for business, complete with pseudo-BR(LMR) totems to announce the location. Note how the previous wall and embankment have been adapted to accommodate the new entry.

Apart from the obvious appearance of the canopy and columns, by 15 September 2012 other changes have been more subtle, but the whole is now a more workmanlike and functional structure, well designed to cope with the demands of travellers and other visitors. *Both MJS*

LEICESTER NORTH: Apart from perhaps having a coffee or taking advantage of the toilet facilities, the periods between trains at Leicester North could be very quiet for visitors, with little to hold the attention. Over time, to address this, there have been occasions when 'spare' locomotives have been rostered to spend time on the old up line running into the very short second platform. Guest of honour on 13 August 1994 is No 46229 *Duchess of Hamilton*, looking truly magnificent in its spotless **LMS 'Crimson Lake'** coat.

Though nowhere near as exciting visually as the 'Duchess', No 42968 still solicits attention on 30 January 2010 as the crew take some time to examine their charge after arrival from a mixed freight from Loughborough during the GCR's 'Lostock & Several Smoking Barrels' three-day gala. *Both MJS*

LEICESTER NORTH: We have literally reached the end of this journey, have left the train and the Leicester North terminus, and now make our way back to our waiting car, parked on the approach road on 14 August 1994. Plans were once mooted to build a likeness of Marylebone here, but thus far that has not materialised.

So near and yet so far... The view to the south from the station, across the 'valley' to the old trackbed on the embankment in the centre distance, looks so tempting, but to travel once more to the former Abbey Lane Sidings would take a massive 'concrete leap' across what was Thurcaston Road and is now a wider Red Hill Way, as well as megabucks and for very little extra value in reality. One can but dream! *Both MJS*